SHAMBHALA
CLASSICS

The Art *of*
Worldly Wisdom

Baltasar Gracián

Adapted from the translation by
JOSEPH JACOBS

With an introduction by
WILLIS BARNSTONE

SHAMBHALA
Boston & London
2000

SHAMBHALA PUBLICATIONS, INC.

HORTICULTURAL HALL

300 MASSACHUSETTS AVENUE

BOSTON, MASSACHUSETTS 02115

www.shambhala.com

9   8   7   6   5   4   3   2   1

Printed in the United States of America
This edition is printed on acid-free paper that meets the
American National Standards Institute z39.48 Standard.
Distributed in the United States by Random House, Inc.,
and in Canada by Random House of Canada Ltd
Cover art: Decorative initial letter, from an
illuminated codex at the monastery of Iveron.

THE LIBRARY OF CONGRESS CATALOGUES THE
PREVIOUS EDITION OF THIS BOOK AS FOLLOWS:
Gracián y Morales, Baltasar, 1601–1658.
[Oráculo manual y arte de prudencia. English]
The art of worldly wisdom/Balthasar Gracián
translated by Joseph Jacobs. —1st Shambhala ed.
p.   cm.—(Shambhala pocket classics)
ISBN 0-87773-921-8 (pbk.: alk. paper)
ISBN 1-57062-745-2 (pbk.)
1. Maxims. I. Title. II. Series.
PQ6398.G307   1993   92-50738
868´.302—dc20   CIP

CONTENTS

INTRODUCTION
Courage of the Word in Gracián's Pen and Life
ℒℙ

WILLIS BARNSTONE
Distinguished Professor of Spanish and
Comparative Literature, Indiana University

Wisdom literatures in the form of cunning aphorisms are universal. Ancient cultures on all continents have them, and they spring up, often as countercultural collections, offering ways of confronting prevailing orthodoxy and providing words for personal survival, dignity, and deliverance. In China we have the spiritual *Daodejing* (*Tao Te Ching*), in ancient Greece Herakleitos' philosophical cosmic fragments, in Aragón near Gracián's birthplace the Latin Martial's satiric barbs, in Israel the poignant skepticism of Ecclesiastes, and among the Gnostics the 144 sayings in the Gospel of Thomas, which in their glimpse of the soul bring us back to the paradoxes of the *Daodejing*.

In recent centuries this old tradition of virtue utterance has shown no sign of declining. La Rochefoucauld's 504 gloomy *maximes morales* (1655) imitated Gracián's elliptical aphorisms. Schopenhauer translated Baltasar Gracián's *The Art of Worldly Wisdom*, transforming the "triumph of the will" from the Jesuit priest's lexicon into the centerpiece of his own *The World as Will and Representation* (1818). In his *Thus Spoke Zarathustra* (1891), Nietzsche, off on his mountain of dissidence, carried the wondrous practice of writing maxims into the twentieth century.

Wisdom sayings are also the salt of popular speech, a source of knowledge for facing every event from birth to death. In modern Greece the ancient Greek maxim persists in impelling one to action: "You may have Athena with you, but move your hands." In Spain the hundreds of aphorisms from Sancho Panza's mouth—mocking person, church, and state—are echoed by the refrains of a modern Andalusian peasant, whose tongue is a lamenting trill, a rhyming dagger, and, when soaring, a dove biting the stars.

Sharp aphorisms pick the mind, look inside to illumine a salvific way, or operate, as many of Gracián's do, to win, with absolute equanimity, an ethical duel. This patient philosopher of pessimism and epiphany very early articulates an Emersonian self-reliance, along with his own sententious word of moderate hope, in a world where enemies and envious fools pop out of the darkness. The Jesuit tells us how to be cool, how to adapt to circumstance, how to survive even when, in his case, his superiors in Rome have forced him into exiled silence for his uncensored speech.

Baltasar Gracián was an aphorist, imaginary biographer, and novelist, who published studies of ideal figures and handbooks on the arts of rhetoric and comportment. These books were *The Hero* (*El héroe*, 1637), an imaginary portrait of a perfect but practical Machiavellian leader; *The Complete Gentleman* (*El discreto*, 1646), a Castiglione-like picture of a sensible gentleman; *Shrewdness and Art of the Artist* (*Agudeza y arte de ingenio*, 1642–48), a manual of poetic wit and conceit; *The Art of Worldly Wisdom* (*Oráculo manual y arte de prudencia*,1647), a handbook of prudent behavior; and *The Master Critic* (*Criticón*, 1651–57), a grave allegorical novel on the bleakness of life that was to cost him his own freedom. All these dynamic secular efforts are a wild mix for a priest-professor of the Jesuit order founded by Saint Ignacio de Loyola. But Gracián was his own worldly self, of and not of his profession, of and not of his time. And in life he was a rebel with militant impulses closer to those of Loyola than to his own cautionary stance that he advocated in *The Art of Worldly Wisdom*. Loyola forged his soldiers of Christ into regiments of clerics to conquer new souls, for which boldness he was in and out of prison; Gracián was in hot water for the acts of writing and publication. He constantly disobeyed orders to conform and be silent. Ultimately, Gracián was targeted by the German general of the order, Goswin Nickel, who hounded him from his post as professor of sacred scripture in the city of Zaragoza into supervised house arrest in the town of Tarazona where, dispirited, angry, and sick, Gracián died. Unlike his teachings, which recommended prudent avoidance of pain and distress, Gracián chose to be an independent man of letters and to be punished. In this paradox of free life and prudent sayings, we will find keys to the antithetical mysteries of his laconic writing.

A look at the author's life tells a curious tale. Baltasar Gracián y Morales was born in 1601 in the village of Belmonte in Aragón, near the city of Calatayud. His father was a doctor. As a young adolescent he went to study in a *colegio* (school or college) in Toledo, the old Spanish capital from the time of the Visigoth kings. El Greco was then painting in Toledo. No two people would seem to be more clearly at opposite poles of temperament and art—El Greco, whose mystical passion fills the large, open eyes of his elongated figures draped in luminous robes, souls rising, and Gracián, whose ideal characters are neatly and properly attired, measured in emotion and imagination as they circumspectly observe targets of influence. The painter and the aphorist are fire and water. Or appear to be. But, to use one of his favorite metaphors, Gracián has secret cards he only occasionally reveals that betray a daring passion and a visceral hope in the face of the darkness of a bad age.

After studying philosophy and letters in Toledo, and perhaps also in Zaragoza, Gracián returned to Aragón and in May 1619 entered the novitiate of the Society of Jesus. He followed the steps of Loyola, who in Spanish is familiarly referred to as Santo Padre Ignacio. He studied philosophy for two years in the Colegio de Calatayud (1621–23) and theology for the next four years in Zaragoza. The Spanish critic Emilio Blanco describes the young scholar, "In this city of Ebro it seems that the young Gracián had already adopted his withdrawn and isolated personality—an attitude of superiority, in a word, that would characterize him—and perhaps there began his literary vocation."[1] Later, in 1627, he was ordained a priest. For the next nine years he taught philosophy at diverse *colegios*, but then he was appointed as confessor and preacher in his native city of Huesca.

This was a pivotal moment, for there in Huesca he not only wrote and published his first book, *The Hero* (1637), but met Vincencio Juan de Lastanosa, who was to be his loyal patron. Lastanosa, a learned and wealthy nobleman six years his junior, had established among his elegant gardens a science museum and an important art gallery that contained paintings by Ribera, Tintoretto, Dürer, and Titian, as well as sculptures of classical antiquity. His library held seven thousand books. His was the salon of northeastern Spain. Lastanosa became Gracián's close friend, financier of his books, and protector in dangerous moments. This was a keen opportunity for the young prelate. He met not only painters and writers but also historians, composers, and scientists. Suspicious of his superiors, and with good reason, he followed his own advice of evasion and dissimulation by publishing *The Hero* without permission from the general of the Jesuit order and under the pseudonym Lorenzo Gracián. The book was a success, going into six editions in seven years, and was presented to Philip IV. However, his pseudonym was not a good disguise and his worldly publications soon got him in trouble. In his third year in Huesca he was sent out of the city.

The next years found the writer-priest in the anomalous position of publishing more books, receiving more attention and prestige as a writer, getting better posts, such as rector of the Jesuit College at Tarragona in 1642, but at the same time he aroused jealousy and fury among his superiors for his frivolous and heretical publications. So the "undisciplined" Gracián found himself being moved to a new position before the normal period of appointment. His reputation in Madrid, which he occasionally visited, grew. He dedicated books to illustrious figures—*El Político* to the duke of Nocera in 1640 and *El Discreto* to the Infante

[1] Emilio Blanco, *Oráculo manual y arte de prudencia* (Madrid: Catedra, 1995), 18.

Baltasar Carlos in 1646. This strategy gave his volumes protection, but his social and literary successes did not give him personal cover. Attacks increased. By now he was notorious enough to be denounced by the general of the Jesuit order in Rome.

In 1646 a French army occupied the Catalan city of Lérida, and a Spanish regiment engaged the French in battles of atrocious slaughter. Gracián's last employer sent him, "with good riddance," to be chaplain with the royal troops under the marquis of Leganés, who freed Lérida. He attended the wounded. In December of the same year he returned to his preferred Huesca, and by the spring of 1647, in that same city, he published *The Art of Worldly Wisdom*. This book is a concise summary, in three hundred pithy paragraphs, of the worldly wisdom that he had accumulated as he fenced his way through a threatened life.

The priest did a balancing act, lining up protectors for each new publishing success that he slipped by the Jesuit eyes. He also had his protectors among the clergy, including the provincial Diego de Alastuey, who though ordered to investigate the priest, protected him and indeed permitted Gracián to retain an excellent post—his professorship of holy scripture at Zaragoza, the capital city. At this time he brought out a religious work, *The Communicant (El comulgatorio)* (1655) that he dedicated to the marquise de Valdueza, the queen's primary lady-in-waiting. He is said to have put out this dull, uncharacteristic work to regain favor with the church authorities. For the first time he had submitted a work for approval and for the first time put it out under his own name. But things only got worse, since *The Communicant* overlapped the three-part publication of his satiric novel *The Master Critic (Criticón)* (1651–57), which attacked the high-placed fools he perceived around him. He drew his characters with the thinnest disguise, and his enemies saw themselves personally attacked. They planned revenge. The second part of *The Master Critic* he dedicated to Don Juan of Austria.

By now Lastanosa himself was drawn into the whispers of fear. Lastanosa was secretly sending trustworthy messengers around with chapters of the book in progress. When the third part of the novel appeared, it was received by Gracián's superiors as an act of open defiance. The provincial of the order, no longer his protector Alastuey but Jacinto Piquer, an enemy, dismissed him from his post at Zaragoza and sentenced him to fast on bread and water. His rooms were watched to prevent him from again picking up pen and paper. Then, somehow, there was a brief reprieve and he was sent on an honorable mission to Alagón, near Zaragoza. But matters worsened when the priest asked to be released from the order to join a mendicant one. For this last offense, Nickel, the general of the order in Rome, sent him to Tarazona. Soon after, on the 6th of December 1658, alone and completely silenced, he died in disgrace.

Some years later, his first college in Calatayud displayed his portrait in their cloister.

The gloom and glory in Baltasar Gracián's life was in keeping with the twilight years in this last segment of Spain's two hundred years of the Golden Age, which is traditionally acknowledged as having begun in 1492. Perhaps the core date of this renaissance in the arts was 1474 when Isabel I ascended the throne of Castile and five years later when her husband Fernando inherited the crown of Aragón. These events at last made it possible to unite Spain politically, linguistically, and religiously. Castilian became the national language. In fact, poetry in Catalan, Galician-Portuguese, Basque, and Gracián's own Aragonese dialect disappeared and was not heard again until the nineteenth century when it emerged as the voice of regional nationalism. The year 1492 changed Spain, the West, and world history. Columbus sailed to the West, looking for East Asia. He found the New World. In the same year, Spanish Jews who had not converted to Christianity were driven from their ancient homes into exile. For Spanish letters the primary event was the publication by the humanist Antonio de Nebrija of *The Art of the Spanish Language (Arte de la lengua castellana)*, the first Spanish grammar and the first systematic grammar of any European language. So 1492 indeed represented not only the dividing year between the Middle Ages and the Renaissance, but the beginning of those two centuries of the arts that Spaniards like to call the Golden Age *(Siglo de oro)*.

The early Golden Age gave us the Renaissance poet Garcilaso de la Vega, the mystical poets Saint John of the Cross (1542–1591) and Fray Luis de León (1527–1591), and Saint Teresa's *Interior Castile* (1577). In the seventeenth century, Spain's novels and plays became the models for later European literatures. The novel reached its zenith with Miguel de Cervantes' *Don Quijote de la Mancha* (1610–15) and Francisco de Quevedo's *The Life of the Swindler* (1626). In the theater were Tirso de Molina's *The Trickster of Seville,* the first Don Juan play (1630), and Calderón de la Barca's *Life Is a Dream,* with its frame of illusion and reality that earlier held together Cervantes' enormous masterpiece. Gracián's century was (if we leave out Saint John of the Cross) the century of Spain's greatest poets, which included Luis de Góngora (1561–1627) and Francisco de Quevedo (1580–1645). Góngora, like Maurice Scève in France, was a magician of the surreally obscure and allusive text, and Quevedo, like his counterpart John Donne in London, was a metaphysical poet whose range, after the breaking of the medieval circle, was the discovered world.

Through conquest and national and cultural unification, Spain had increased its hegemony and wealth, but its "purification" of religion and people within the country soon led to a poverty of cultural isolation and economic backwardness. After two centuries Spain was exhausted. The signs were everywhere. The nation had been living off New World gold, it had thrown out the working and mercantile class of Jews and Moors, it had lost its vast European territories, and had seen the French invading its northern region. After a succession of weak kings in a court attended by corrupt officials, recovery was doomed. The economy plunged, causing sporadic famine and inciting the picaresque novellas of hunger. All these known and often repeated causes of Spain's decline entered the vocabulary of its best authors, including that of the Mexican nun Sor Juana Inés de la Cruz, the great figure among New World writers of the sixteenth, seventeenth, and eighteenth centuries in the Americas. Like Gracián she was sentenced to silence. In her case it was the bishop of Puebla who castigated her inappropriate secular books. She answered his letter warning her to desist with her *Response to Sor Filotea* (1691), an autobiographical *Room of One's Own* in which she asserts her intellectual and creative freedom, her right to write and to publish, and her refutation of all censorial intrusion. However, after the rebuke from the bishop, she ceased writing and sold her library. Shortly thereafter she died while attending her sister nuns during a plague that had reached their Hieronymite convent. The bishop's letter served to mute her voice in precisely the same way as envious authorities had ordered Seneca and Gracián into silence.

The Spanish priest and the Mexican nun, without family resources, in need of a benefactor and employer, had found their way into the church. Life was a risk, and even Saint John of the Cross and Miguel de Cervantes, both descendants of *conversos* (Jews compelled to convert to Christianity), found themselves in and out of prison. Saint John of the Cross had no pen with which to write his *Dark Night of the Soul* during the nine months he was locked in a sardine closet in a rival Carmelite monastery in Toledo. Quevedo, an old Castilian nobleman, ended his life in a lightless dungeon when his protector fell out of favor. He asked for pen and paper and light. It was essentially the same request that William Tyndale, first translator of the Bible into vernacular English, made of his Belgian captors before they took him to the stake, strangled him, and set him on fire in 1536. He had asked for a lamp, a pen, the Hebrew Bible, and a Hebrew dictionary to continue his work. The Jesuit Gracián was ordered to a room where, under supervision, he was forbidden to touch pen to paper, a sentence in force until his death.

But risk and punishment notwithstanding, the arts in Spain flourished, reaching their fullness at moments of darkening peril. We see a judgment of these twilight times in a sonnet by the master poet of Europe, Francisco de Quevedo:

He Shows How All Things Warn of Death

I gazed upon my country's tottering walls,
one day grandiose, now rubble on the ground,
worn out by vicious time, only renowned
for weakness in a land where courage fails.
I went into the fields. I saw the sun
drinking the springs just melted from the ice,
and cattle moaning as the forests climb
against the thinning day, now overrun
with shade. I went into my house. I saw
my old room yellowed with the sickening breath
of age, my cane flimsier than before.
I felt my sword coffined in rust, and walked
about, and everything I looked at bore
a warning of the wasted gaze of death.[2]

The Jesuit Gracián's most elegant answer to his times is his handbook of worldly wisdom. It is no wonder that this stubborn, aloof, even contemptuous author seems at times to be himself soulless, with no hermetic refuge for hidden spirit, since so many of his three hundred wisdom sayings are addressed to survival in a world that might break him. Of the three hundred maxims it should first be observed that seventy-two of them appeared in almost the same form in his earlier works, suggesting that his preoccupation with survival was not new. And were they really maxims? In the epigrammatic tradition, maxims or aphorisms usually consist of one or two sentences, as in the old Spanish saying, *en boca cerrada no entran moscas,* "in a closed mouth flies don't enter." Gracián's aphorisms are short elliptical paragraphs, more like Montaigne's meditations on a theme, although they are briefer and his sentences are militantly short. This brevity and use of the naked line is wholly uncharacteristic in these last years of the florid Spanish *baroco.*

[2] Willis Barnstone, *Six Masters of the Spanish Sonnet* (Carbondale, Ill.: Southern Illinois University Press, 1993), 33.

Against those who would harm him, Gracián's first line of defense in his sayings is a stoic acceptance of wickedness, a theme familiar to his fellow Spaniard from Córdoba, Seneca the younger (4 B.C.E-65 C.E.), who wrote his Latin essays on anger, Stoic impassivity, and the peace of the soul in Rome while tutoring mad Nero. After Nero's death, the emperor's widow demanded Seneca's death, which brought momentary silence to his voice. Gracián alludes to Seneca in his sorrowful maxim entitled "Reality and Appearance." He writes, "Things pass for what they seem, not for what they are. Few see inside, many get attached to appearances. It is not enough to be right if your actions look false and ill" (99). Elsewhere he tells us that given the ill around him, it is best not to reveal too much (260), and he goes on to give the following instructions: "do not show your wounded finger" (145), "never have a companion who outshines you" (152), "rely on yourself" (167), "know the great people of your age" (203), "never act out of passion" (287), and "surfeits of happiness are fatal" (200).

Then, after 299 paragraphs of caution and hidden spiritual escapes, the priests tells us, curiously, to "be a saint" (300). His sayings evoke neither a saint nor a martyr. But in life he was a fighter getting his word out at whatever cost, including his life. And yes, he was a virtuous artist. After the implausible religious pitch for sainthood, another sop perhaps for authorities, the same maxim ends bravely with a writer's hope of fame and remembrance. Earlier in his text he had contrasted enduring fame with the shallow temporality of fortune during one's life. He concludes *The Art of Worldly Wisdom* by writing,

> Virtue is the sun of our world, and has for its course a good conscience. She is so beautiful that she finds favor with both God and man. Nothing is lovable but virtue, nothing detestable but vice. A person's capacity and greatness are to be measured by his virtue, not by his fortune. She alone is all-sufficient. She makes people lovable in life, memorable after death. (300)

Around 600 B.C.E. Sappho also said, "Someone, I tell you / will remember us."[3] And Schopenhauer, with his translation of Gracián's handbook of wisdom, indeed remembered. In *Litteraische Notiz vor seine Übersetzung,* the philosopher wrote his endorsement of the author he so esteemed:

> It would possibly be rather difficult to disprove the thesis that the Spanish nation has produced the best maxims of practical wisdom, the best proverb, the best epitaph, and the best motto in the world. . . . To read it [*The Art of Worldly Wisdom*] once through is obviously not enough; it is a book made for constant use as occasion serves—in short, to be a companion for life.[4]

There remains an enigma in the work of Gracián. Is it mere cynicism of a noble nature that has made the author so dismissive of fools, so ready to withhold passion and information from adversaries in order to trump them or at least hold them off? Will a great spirit advise us, as Gracián does in maxim 94, to mix a little mystery with everything, or to keep one's imagination and intentions shielded in armor, and to keep the extent of our abilities unknown? Is the world really divided between fools and knaves? These are Gracián's thoughts, and to deny them is to deny evidence of an internal tragedy. An abuse of soul is clear when one looks closer at the other lines of worldly advice that seem to threaten this armored posture. In these lines we find a discreet message, evident in his life, of courage, patience, dignity, refuge in one's own soul, and the certainty that enforced silence will not hush honor and truth. Gracián felicitously particularizes these generalizations in his gracious metaphors. They are the author's deliverance. After so much defensive and conformist speech to the vulnerable, his own vulnerability comes like a sweet breeze to a climber laughing on his mountain. These

---

[3] Willis Barnstone, *Sappho, Poems: A New Version* (Los Angeles: Green Interger, 1999), 139.
[4] Sir M. E. Grant Druff, "Baltasar Gracián," *Fortnightly Review,* March 1877, 328.

insights allow us to pause, to understand his rhetorical grievance, and to enter, unsentimentally—he is never a sobbing sentimentalist—into the stoic strength and beauty of Gracián's otherness.

Suddenly we learn about friendship, that it is all that counts in dealing with the world. Not about useful and great friends, but about the good ones whom one keeps. He writes with succinct power:

> Keeping friends is more important than making them. Select those that wear well—if they are new at first it is some consolation that they will become old. Absolutely the best are those well salted, though they may require soaking in the testing. There is no desert like living without friends. Friendship multiplies the good of life and divides the evil. It is the sole remedy against misfortune, like fresh air to the soul. (158)

In the same vein, the beleaguered Jesuit tells us that "moral courage exceeds physical courage" (54), and that we must "know how to wait. It is a sign of a noble heart to be endowed with patience" (55). And he also informs us about what really endures:

> Be slow and sure. Things are done quickly enough if done well. If just quickly done they can be quickly undone. To last an eternity requires an eternity of preparation. Only excellence counts, only achievement endures. Profound intelligence is the only foundation for immortality. What is worth much costs much. The precious metals are the heaviest. (57)

In the end he subverts all his worldly maxims of survival when he speaks about moving toward integrity come hell or high water. According to him you must not fear what others say, even if you pay fatally for your independence. In a few words Gracián grimly deconstructs his artifice and the arsenal of tricks and postures that he has been recommending. In keeping with his nonconformist life, and with poignant courage, he informs us that even in the worst of times,

Never lose your self-respect. And do not be too self-conscious. Let your own integrity be the true standard of your rectitude, and let your own self-judgment be more strict than all external laws. Avoid anything unseemly more from regard for your own self-respect than from fear of external authority. Pay regard to that and there is no need of Seneca's imaginary monitor [i.e., one's conscience]. (50)

You should not tire of Baltasar Gracián. There is surprise under surprise. He is to be reread, as good work always is, rather than discarded. He gives us advice there, too, for he tells us "Do not be a bore. . . . Good things, when short, are twice as good" (105).

The Art *of* Worldly Wisdom

· 1 ·

EVERYTHING IS AT ITS PEAK OF PERFECTION. This is especially true of the art of making one's way in the world. There is more required nowadays to make a single wise person than formerly to make the Seven Sages of ancient Greece, and more is needed nowadays to deal with a single person than was required with a whole people in former times.

· 2 ·

CHARACTER AND INTELLECT. These are the two poles of our capacity; one without the other is but halfway to happiness. Intellect is not enough, character is also needed. On the other hand, it is the fool's misfortune to fail in obtaining the position, employment, neighborhood, and circle of friends of his choice.

· 3 ·

KEEP MATTERS FOR A TIME IN SUSPENSE. Admiration at their novelty heightens the value of your achievements. It is both useless and insipid to play with your cards on the table. If you do not declare yourself immediately, you arouse expectation, especially when the importance of your position makes you the object of general attention. Mix a little mystery with everything, and the very mystery arouses veneration. And when you explain, do not be too explicit, just as you do not expose your inmost thoughts in ordinary conversation. Cautious silence is the sacred sanctuary of worldly wisdom. A resolution declared is never highly thought of—it only leaves room for criticism. And if it happens to fail, you are doubly unfortunate. Besides, you imitate the divine way when you inspire people to wonder and watch.

· 4 ·

KNOWLEDGE AND COURAGE. These are the elements of greatness. Because they are immortal they bestow immortality. Each is as much as he knows, and the wise can do anything. A person without knowledge is in a world without light. Wisdom and strength are the eyes and hands. Knowledge without courage is sterile.

· 5 ·

MAKE PEOPLE DEPEND ON YOU. It is not he that adorns but he that adores that makes a divinity. The wise person would rather see others needing him than thanking him. To keep them on the threshold of hope is diplomatic, to trust to their gratitude is boorish; hope has a good memory, gratitude a bad one. More is to be got from dependence than from courtesy. He that has satisfied his thirst turns his back on the well, and the orange once squeezed falls from the golden platter into the waste basket. When dependence disappears good behavior goes with it, as well as respect. Let it be one of the chief lessons of experience to keep hope alive without entirely satisfying it, by preserving it to make oneself always needed, even by a patron on the throne. But do not carry silence to excess or you will go wrong, nor let another's failing grow incurable for the sake of your own advantage.

· 6 ·

A PERSON AT HIS PEAK. We are not born perfect. Every day we develop in our personality and in our profession until we reach the highest point of our completed being, to the full round of our accomplishments and of our excellences. This is known by the purity of our taste, the clearness of our thought, the maturity of our judgment, and the firmness of our will. Some never arrive at being complete—something is always lacking. Others ripen late. The complete person—wise in speech, prudent in act—is admitted to the familiar intimacy of discreet people and is even sought out by them.

· 7 ·

AVOID OUTSHINING YOUR SUPERIORS. All victories breed hate, and that over your superior is foolish or fatal. Preeminence is always detested, especially over those who are in high positions. Caution can gloss over common advantages. For example, good looks may be cloaked by careless attire. There are some that will grant you superiority in good luck or good temper, but none in good sense, least of all a prince—for good sense is a royal prerogative and any claim of superiority in that is a crime against majesty. They are princes, and wish to be so in that most princely of qualities. They will allow someone to help them but not to surpass them. So make any advice given to them appear like a recollection of something they have only forgotten rather than as a guide to something they cannot find. The stars teach us this finesse with happy tact: though they are his children and brilliant like him, they never rival the brilliance of the sun.

· 8 ·

BE WITHOUT PASSIONS. This is the highest quality of the mind. Its very eminence redeems us from being affected by transient and low impulses. There is no higher rule than that over oneself, over one's impulses; there is the triumph of free will. When passion rules your character do not let it threaten your position, especially if it is a high one. It is the only refined way of avoiding trouble and the shortest way back to a good reputation.

· 9 ·

AVOID THE FAULTS OF YOUR NATION. Water shares the good or bad qualities of the channels through which it flows and people share those of the climate in which they are born. Some owe more than others to their native land, because there is a more favorable sky in the zenith. There is not a nation among even the most civilized that has not some fault peculiar to itself that other nations blame by way of boast or as a warning. It is a triumph of cleverness to correct in oneself such failings, or even to hide them. You get great credit for being unique among your fellows because what is less expected is esteemed all the more. There are also family failings as well as faults of position, of office, or of age. If these all meet in one person and are not carefully guarded against, they make an intolerable monster.

· 10 ·

FORTUNE AND FAME. Where the one is fickle the other is enduring. The first is for this life, the second for the next; fortune against envy, fame against oblivion. Fortune is desired, and sometimes nurtured, but fame is earned. The desire for fame springs from virtue. Fame was and is the sister of the giants; it always goes to extremes—either horrible monsters or brilliant prodigies.

· 11 ·

CULTIVATE RELATIONSHIPS WITH THOSE WHO CAN TEACH YOU. Let friendly intercourse be a school of knowledge, and let culture be taught through conversation. Thus you make your friends your teachers and mingle the pleasures of conversation with the advantages of instruction. Sensible people enjoy alternating pleasures: you are rewarded with applause for what you say and you gain instruction from what you hear. We are always attracted to others by our own interest, but in this case it is of a higher kind. Wise people frequent the houses of great nobility as theatres of heroism not temples of vanity. They are renowned for their worldly wisdom, not only for being oracles of all nobleness by their example and their behavior, but because those who surround them form a courtly academy of worldly wisdom of the best and noblest kind.

· 12 ·

NATURE AND ART, MATERIAL AND WORKMANSHIP. There is no beauty unadorned and no excellence that would not become barbaric if it were not supported by artifice. This remedies the bad and improves the good. Nature scarcely ever gives us the very best—for that we must have recourse to art. Without this the best of natural dispositions remains uncultured, lacking half its excellence if training is absent. Everyone has something unrefined that needs training, and every kind of excellence needs some polish.

· 13 ·

ACT SOMETIMES ON SECOND THOUGHTS, SOMETIMES ON FIRST IM-PULSE. Life is a warfare against the malice of others. Sagacity fights with strategic changes of intention—never doing what it threatens, aiming only to escape notice. It aims in the air with dexterity and strikes home in an unexpected direction, always seeking to conceal its game. It lets a purpose appear in order to attract the opponent's attention, but then turns round and conquers by the unexpected. But a penetrating intelligence anticipates this by watchfulness and lurks in ambush. It always understands the opposite of what the opponent wishes it to understand, and recognizes every feint of guile. It lets the first impulse pass by and waits for the second, or even the third. Sagacity now rises to higher flights on seeing its artifice foreseen: It tries to deceive by truth itself, changing its game in order to change its deceit, cheats by not cheating, and bases its deception on the greatest candor. But the opposing intelligence is on guard with increased watchfulness and discovers the darkness concealed by the light and deciphers every move, the more subtle because more simple. In this way the guile of the Python combats the far darting rays of Apollo.*

· 14 ·

THE THING ITSELF AND THE WAY IT IS DONE. *Substance* is not enough, attention to *circumstance* is also required. A bad manner spoils everything—even reason and justice—a good one supplies everything, gilds, even sweetens truth, and adds a touch of beauty to old age itself. The *how* plays a large part in affairs, a good manner steals people's hearts. Fine behavior is a joy in life, and a pleasant expression can help you out of a difficult situation in a remarkable way.

· 15 ·

KEEP AUXILIARY WITS AROUND YOU. It is a privilege of the powerful to surround themselves with the champions of intellect who protect them from the dangers of every ignorance, who untangle them from the snarls of every difficulty. It is a rare greatness to know how to make use of the wise; it far exceeds the barbarous taste of Tigranes,† who delighted in enslaving kings as his servants. It is a novel kind of supremacy—the best that life can offer—to use skill to make as servants of those who by nature are our masters. It is a great thing to know, little to live; there is no real life without knowledge. There is remarkable cleverness in studying without effort, in getting much by means of many, and through them all to become wise. Afterwards, you speak in the council chamber on behalf of many, and since as many sages speak through your mouth as were consulted beforehand you thus obtain the fame of an oracle by others' efforts. Such auxiliary wits distill the best books

* In Greek mythology, Apollo shot Python with arrows at the foot of Mount Parnassus—Ed.
† Tigranes (c.140–55 B.C.E.), King of Armenia, had conquests across Asia Minor, and was in the habit of having the leaders of his vanquished foes appear in public with him.—Ed.

and serve up the quintessence of wisdom. He that cannot have sages in service should have them for his friends.

· 16 ·

KNOWLEDGE AND GOOD INTENTIONS. Together they ensure continued success. A fine intellect wedded to a wicked will is always an unnatural monster. A wicked will poisons all perfections; helped by knowledge it only ruins with greater subtlety. It is a miserable superiority that only results in ruin. Knowledge without sense is double folly.

· 17 ·

VARY YOUR MODE OF ACTION. So as to distract attention, do not always do things the same way, especially if you have a rival. Do not always act on first impulse; people will soon recognize the uniformity and, by anticipating, frustrate your designs. It is easy to kill a bird on the wing that flies straight, not so one that twists and turns. Nor should you always act on second thoughts; people will discern the plan the second time. The enemy is on the watch, great skill is required to outwit him. The gamester never plays the card the opponent expects, still less the one he wants.

· 18 ·

APPLICATION AND ABILITY. There is no attaining eminence without both, and where they unite there is the greatest fame. Mediocre people obtain more with application than superior people without it. Work is the price that is paid for reputation. What costs little is of little worth. Even for the highest posts it is only in some cases application that is wanting, rarely the talent. To prefer moderate success in great things over eminence in a humble post may be excused by a generous mind, but there is no excuse for being content with humble mediocrity when you could shine among the highest. Thus nature and art are both needed, and application makes them complete.

· 19 ·

AROUSE NO EXAGGERATED EXPECTATIONS WHEN YOU START SOME-THING. It is the misfortune of all celebrated people not to fulfill afterwards the expectations beforehand formed of them. The real can never equal the imagined, for it is easy to form ideals but very difficult to realize them. Imagination weds hope and gives birth to much more than things are in themselves. However excellent something is, it never suffices to fulfill expectations. And as people find themselves disappointed with their exorbitant expectations they are more readily disillusioned than impressed. Hope is a great falsifier of truth; let skill guard against this by ensuring that fruition exceeds desire. A few creditable attempts at the beginning are sufficient to arouse curiosity without pledging one to the final object. It is better that reality should surpass the design and it turns out better than was thought. This rule does not apply to wicked things, for the same exaggeration is a great aid with them and draws general applause; what seemed at first extreme ruin comes to be thought of as quite bearable.

· 20 ·

A MAN OF THE TIMES. The rarest individuals depend on their times. It is not everyone that finds the times he deserves, and even when he finds it he does not always know how to utilize it. Some people have been worthy of a better century, for every species of good does not always triumph. Things have their period—even excellent qualities are subject to fashion. Wisdom has one advantage: she is immortal. If *this* is not her century many others will be.

· 21 ·

THE ART OF BEING LUCKY. There are rules of luck and the wise do not leave it all to chance. Luck can be assisted by care. Some content themselves with placing themselves confidently at the gate of fortune, waiting till she opens it. Others do better, and press forward and profit by their clever boldness, reaching the goddess and winning her favor on the wings of their virtue and valor. But a true philosophy has no other umpire than virtue and insight—for there is no good or bad luck except wisdom and foolishness.

· 22 ·

KNOWLEDGE HAS A PURPOSE. Wise people arm themselves with tasteful and elegant erudition—a practical and expert knowledge of what is going on, not common gossip. They possess a copious store of wise and witty sayings, and of noble deeds, and know how to employ them at the right moment. Often, more is taught by a jest than by the most serious teaching. Knowledge gained in conversation can be of more help than the seven arts, however liberal.

· 23 ·

BE FREE OF IMPERFECTION. Few live without some weak point, either physical or moral, which they pamper even though they could easily cure it. The keenness of others often regrets to see a slight defect attaching itself to a whole assembly of elevated qualities, and yet a single cloud can hide the whole of the sun. There are likewise blemishes on our reputation, which those with ill will soon discover and continually point out. The highest skill is to transform them into ornament. So Caesar hid his natural defect [of baldness] with the laurel.

· 24 ·

KEEP YOUR IMAGINATION UNDER CONTROL. You must sometimes correct it, sometimes assist it. For it is all important for our happiness and balances reason. The imagination can tyrannize, not being content with looking on, but influences and even often dominates our life. It can make us happy or burden us, depending on the folly that it leads us to. It can make us either content or discontent with ourselves. Before some people it continually holds up the penalties of action and becomes the mortifying lash of fools. To others the imagination promises happiness and adventure with blissful delusion. It can do all this unless you lord over it with the most prudent self-control.

· 25 ·

KNOW HOW TO TAKE A HINT. It was once the art of arts to be able to discourse, now it is no longer sufficient. We must know how to take a hint, especially in disabusing ourselves. You cannot make yourself understood if you do not easily understand others. There are some who act like diviners of the heart and lynxes of intentions. The very truths that concern us most are only half spoken, but with attention we can grasp the whole meaning. When you hear anything favorable keep a tight rein on your credulity; if unfavorable, give it the spur.

· 26 ·

FIND OUT EACH PERSON'S THUMBSCREW. This is the art of setting their wills in action. It needs more skill than resolution. You must know where to get at anyone. Every volition has a special motive that varies according to taste. All people idolize something; for some it is fame, for others self-interest, for most it is pleasure. Skill consists in knowing these idols in order to bring them into play. Know a person's mainspring of motive and you have as it were the key to his will. Have resort to primary motives, which are not always the highest but more often the lowest part of his nature because there are more dispositions badly organized than well. First guess a person's ruling passion, appeal to it with words, set it in motion by temptation, and you will always checkmate his freedom of will.

· 27 ·

PRIZE INTENSITY MORE THAN EXTENT. Excellence resides in quality not in quantity. The best is always few and rare—abundance lowers value. Even among men, the giants are usually really dwarfs. Some reckon books by the thickness, as if they were written to exercise the brawn more than the brain. Extent alone never rises above mediocrity; it is the misfortune of universal geniuses that in attempting to be at home everywhere are so nowhere. Intensity gives eminence and rises to the heroic in matters sublime.

· 28 ·

BE COMMON IN NOTHING. Especially not in taste. It is great and wise to be ill at ease when your deeds please the mob! The excesses of popular applause never satisfy the sensible. There are chameleons of popularity who find enjoyment not in the sweet savors of Apollo but in the breath of the mob. Secondly, do not be common in intelligence; take no pleasure in the wonder of the mob, for ignorance never gets beyond wonder. While vulgar folly wonders, wisdom watches for the deception.

· 29 ·

BE A PERSON OF INTEGRITY. Cling to righteousness with such tenacity of purpose that neither the passions of the mob nor the violence of the tyrant can ever cause you to transgress the bounds of right. But who can be such a phoenix of equity? What a scanty following rectitude has! Many praise it indeed, but few devote themselves. Others follow it until danger threatens; then the false deny it and the politic conceal it. For righteousness cares not if it conflicts with friendship, power, or even self-interest; then comes the danger of desertion. Astute people make plausible distinctions so as not to stand in the way of their superiors or of reasons of state. But straightforward and constant people regard deception as a kind of treason and set more store in tenacity than on sagacity. Such people are always to be found on the side of truth, and if they desert a group they do not change due to fickleness but because the others have first deserted truth.

· 30 ·

HAVE NOTHING TO DO WITH DISREPUTABLE OCCUPATIONS. And have still less to do with fads that bring more notoriety than good reputation. There are many fanciful sects, and the prudent person flees from them all. There are people with bizarre tastes that always take to heart every-thing that wise people repudiate. They live in love with eccentricity, and this may make them well known indeed but more as an object of ridicule than of good reputation. A cautious person does not make public his pursuit of wisdom, still less those matters that make him or his followers seem ridiculous. These need not be specified—common contempt has sufficiently singled them out.

· 31 ·

SELECT THE LUCKY AND AVOID THE UNLUCKY. Bad luck is generally the penalty of folly and for the unfortunate there is no disease so conta-gious. Never open the door to a lesser evil, for other and greater ones will invariably slink in after it. The greatest skill at cards is to know when to discard; the smallest of current trumps is worth more than the ace of trumps of the last game. When in doubt, follow the suit of the wise and prudent—sooner or later they will win the odd trick.

· 32 ·

HAVE A REPUTATION FOR BEING GRACIOUS. It is the chief glory of the high and mighty to be gracious, a prerogative of kings to conquer with universal goodwill. That is the great advantage of a commanding position—to be able to do more good than others. Those make friends who do friendly acts. On the other hand, there are some who fix themselves on not being gracious, not on account of the difficulty but due to a bad disposition. In all things they are the opposite of divine grace.

· 33 ·

KNOW HOW TO WITHDRAW. If it is a great lesson in life to know how to deny, it is still greater to know how to deny oneself as regards both affairs and persons. There are extraneous occupations that eat away precious time. To be occupied in what does not concern you is worse than doing nothing. It is not enough for a careful person not to interfere with others, he must see that they do not interfere with him. One is not obliged to belong so much to others as not to belong at all to oneself. So with friends, their help should not be abused or more demanded from them than they themselves will grant. All excess is a failing, but above all in personal relationships. A wise moderation in this best preserves the goodwill and esteem for all, for by this means that precious boon of courtesy is not gradually worn away. Thus you preserve your genius and freedom to select the best and never sin against the unwritten laws of good taste.

· 34 ·

KNOW YOUR STRONGEST QUALITY. Know your preeminent gift—cultivate it and it will assist the rest. Everyone would have excelled in something if he had known his strong point. Notice in what quality you surpass and take charge of that. In some people judgment excels, in others valor. Most do violence to their natural aptitude and thus attain superiority in nothing. Time enlightens us too late of what was first only a flattering of the passions.

· 35 ·

THINK THINGS OVER, ESPECIALLY THOSE THAT ARE MOST IMPORTANT. All fools come to grief from lack of thought. They never see even the half of things and, as they do not observe their own loss or gain, still less do they apply any diligence to them. Some make much of what matters little and little of much, always weighing in the wrong scale. Many never lose their common sense, because they have none to lose. There are matters that should be observed with the closest attention, and thereafter always kept well in mind. The wise person thinks over everything, but with a difference, most profoundly where there is some profound difficulty, suspecting that perhaps there is more in it than he first thought. Thus his comprehension extends as far as his apprehension.

· 36 ·

BEFORE ACTING OR REFRAINING, WEIGH YOUR LUCK. More depends on that than on noticing your temperament. If he is a fool who at forty applies to Hippocrates for health, still more is he one who only then first applies to Seneca for wisdom. It is a great piece of skill to know how to guide your luck even while waiting for it. For something is accomplished by just waiting to use it at the proper moment, since it has periods and offers opportunities—though one cannot calculate its path because its steps are so irregular. When you find fortune favorable, stride boldly forward, for she favors the bold and, being a woman, the young. But if you have bad luck, withdraw so as not to redouble the influence of your unlucky star.

· 37 ·

KEEP A STORE OF SARCASMS AND KNOW HOW TO USE THEM. This is the point of greatest tact in human intercourse. Such sarcasms are often thrown out to test people's moods, and by their means one often obtains the most subtle and penetrating touchstone of the heart. Other sarcasms are malicious, insolent, poisoned by envy or envenomed by passion, unexpected flashes that destroy at once all favor and esteem. Struck by the slightest word of this kind, many fall away from the closest intimacy with superiors or inferiors that would not have been the slightest shaken by a whole conspiracy of popular insinuation or private malevolence. Other sarcasms work favorably, confirming and assisting one's reputation. But the greater the skill with which they are launched, the greater the caution with which they should be anticipated and received. For here a knowledge of malice is in itself a means of defense, and a shot foreseen always misses its mark.

· 38 ·

LEAVE YOUR LUCK WHILE STILL WINNING. All the best players do it. A fine retreat is as good as a gallant attack. Bring your exploits under cover when there are enough, or even when there are many of them. Luck too long lasting is always suspicious; alternating luck seems safer, and is even sweeter to the taste for a little infusion of bittersweet. The higher the heap of luck, the greater the risk of a slip, and down comes all. Fortune pays you sometimes for the intensity of her favors by the shortness of their duration. She soon tires of carrying anyone long on her shoulders.

· 39 ·

RECOGNIZE WHEN THINGS ARE RIPE, AND KNOW HOW TO ENJOY THEM. The works of nature all reach a certain point of maturity—up to then they improve, then they degenerate. Few works of art reach such a point that they cannot be improved. It is a special privilege of good taste to enjoy everything at its ripest. Not everyone can do this, nor do all who can know how. There is a ripening point too for fruits of intellect, but it is important to know how to recognize it in order to both value it and use it.

· 40 ·

GAIN PEOPLE'S GOODWILL. It is a great thing to gain universal admiration, but greater to gain universal affection. It depends on natural disposition but more so on practice; the first is the foundation, the second then builds on that. Great gifts are not enough, though they are thought to be essential—win good opinion and it is easy to win goodwill. Kindly acts are required to produce kindly feelings—do good with both hands, good words and better deeds, love so as to be loved. Courtesy is the politic magic of great people. First, lay the hand on deeds and then on the pen—words follow swords and the goodwill to be won among writers is eternal.

· 41 ·

NEVER EXAGGERATE. It is an important object of attention not to talk in superlatives, so as neither to offend truth nor cast doubt on your understanding. Exaggeration wastes distinctions and shows the narrowness of one's knowledge or taste. Praise arouses lively curiosity, begets desire, and if afterwards the value does not correspond to the price—as generally happens—expectation revolts against the deception and revenges itself by cheapening both the thing praised and the praiser. A prudent person goes more cautiously to work and prefers to err by understatement than by overstatement. Extraordinary things are rare, therefore temper your evaluation. Exaggeration is akin to lying, and you jeopardize your reputation for good taste and—much worse—good sense.

· 42 ·

NATURAL LEADERSHIP. It is a secret force of superiority not to have to get on by artful trickery but by an inborn power of rule. All submit to it without knowing why, recognizing the secret vigor of natural authority. Such magisterial spirits are kings by merit and lions by innate privilege. By the esteem that they inspire, they hold the hearts and minds of those around them. If their other qualities permit, such people are born to be the prime movers of the state. They perform more by a gesture than others by a long harangue.

· 43 ·

THINK WITH THE FEW AND SPEAK WITH THE MANY. Swimming against the stream makes it is impossible to remove error and easy to fall into danger—only a Socrates can undertake it. To dissent from others' views is regarded as an insult, because it is a condemnation of their judgment. The offense is doubled on account of the judgment condemned and of the person who championed it. Truth is for the few, error is both common and vulgar. The wise person is not known by what he says on the public square, for there he speaks not with his own voice but with that of common folly, however much his inmost thoughts may deny it. The prudent person avoids being contradicted as much as he avoids contradicting others—though they have their judgment ready they are not ready to publish it. Thought is free, force cannot and should not be used on it. The wise person therefore retires into silence and if he allows himself to come out of it, he does so in the shade and before few and fit persons.

· 44 ·

SYMPATHY WITH GREAT MINDS. It is a heroic quality to agree with heroes. It is like a miracle of nature both because of its mystery and for its usefulness. There is a natural kinship of hearts and minds; its effects are such that vulgar ignorance attributes it to magic potions. Esteem and goodwill follow and at times reach affection. It persuades without words and obtains without earning. This sympathy is sometimes active, sometimes passive; both bring great happiness—the more so, the more sublime. It is a great art to recognize, to distinguish, and to utilize this gift. No amount of energy suffices without that favor of nature.

· 45 ·

USE, BUT DO NOT ABUSE, CUNNING. One ought not to delight in it, still less to boast of it. Everything artificial should be concealed, most of all cunning, which is hated. Deceit is common, so our caution has to be redoubled, but not so as to show itself, for caution arouses distrust, causes annoyance, awakens revenge, and gives rise to more ills than you would imagine. To go to work with caution is of great advantage in action, and there is no greater proof of wisdom. The greatest skill in any deed consists in the sure mastery with which it is executed.

· 46 ·

MASTER YOUR ANTIPATHIES. We often allow ourselves to form dislikes of people, even before we know anything about them. At times this innate yet vulgar aversion attaches itself to eminent people. Good sense masters this feeling, for there is nothing more discreditable than to dislike those better than ourselves. As sympathy with great people ennobles us, so dislike of them degrades us.

· 47 ·

AVOID INCURRING OBLIGATIONS. This is one of the chief aims of prudence. People of great ability keep extremes far apart, so that there is a long distance between them. They always keep in the middle of their caution, so they take time to act. It is easier to avoid committing yourself to something than it is to come out of it well. Such affairs test our judgment—it is better to avoid them than to conquer in them. One obligation leads to another and may lead to an affair of dishonor. There are people so constituted by nature or by nation that they easily enter upon such obligations. But for those who walk by the light of reason, such matters require long thinking over. There is more valor needed not to take up the affair than in conquering in it. When there is one fool ready for the occasion, one may excuse oneself from being the second.

· 48 ·

SO MUCH DEPENDS ON BEING A PERSON OF DEPTH. The interior must be at least as impressive as the exterior. Some people's character is all facade, like houses that, due to lack of means, have the portico of a palace leading to the rooms of a cottage. It is no use boring into such people—although they will bore you—because conversation flags after the first salutation. They prance through the first compliments like Sicilian stallions, but silence quickly follows, for the flow of words soon ceases where there is no spring of thoughts. Others may be taken in by them because they themselves have superficial views, but not the prudent, who look within them and find nothing there except material for scorn.

· 49 ·

BE A PERSON OF OBSERVATION AND JUDGMENT. Such a person rules things, not they him. He quickly plumbs the most profound depths. He knows how to get at the anatomy of character. On seeing a person he understands him and judges his inmost nature. From a few observations he deciphers what is most hidden. Keen observation, subtle insight, judicious inference—with these he discovers, notices, grasps, and comprehends everything.

· 50 ·

NEVER LOSE YOUR SELF-RESPECT. And do not be too self-conscious. Let your own integrity be the true standard of your rectitude, and let your own self-judgment be more strict than all external laws. Avoid anything unseemly more from regard for your own self-respect than from fear of external authority. Pay regard to that and there is no need of Seneca's imaginary monitor [i.e., one's conscience].

· 51 ·

KNOW HOW TO CHOOSE WELL. Most of life depends on this. You need good taste and correct judgment, for which neither intellect nor study suffices. To be choice, you must choose well, and for this two things are needed: to be able to choose at all, and then to choose the best. There are many people with fertile and subtle minds, of keen judgment, of much learning, and of great observation who still are at a loss when they come to choosing. They always take the worst as if they were determined to go wrong. Thus, knowing how to choose well is one of the greatest gifts.

· 52 ·

NEVER BE UPSET. It is a great aim of prudence never to be embarrassed. This is the sign of a real person, of a noble heart, for magnanimity is not easily put off balance. The passions are the humors of the soul, and every excess in them weakens prudence. If they overflow through the mouth, the reputation will be in danger. Let us therefore be so great a master over ourselves that neither in the most fortunate nor in the most adverse circumstances can anything cause our reputation injury by disturbing our self-possession, but rather enhance it by showing superiority.

· 53 ·

BE DILIGENT AND INTELLIGENT. Diligence promptly executes what intelligence carefully thought through. Haste is the failing of fools—they know not the obstacles and set to work without preparation. On the other hand, the wise more often fail from procrastination—foresight begets deliberation, and delay often nullifies prompt judgment. Promptness is the mother of good fortune. He has done much who leaves nothing until tomorrow. "Make haste slowly" is a magnificent motto.

· 54 ·

KNOW HOW TO SHOW YOUR STRENTGH. Even hares can pull the mane of a dead lion. Courage is no joking matter. Give way to the first and you must yield to the second, and so on till the last, and to gain your point in the end costs as much trouble as it would have at first. Moral courage exceeds physical courage; it should be like a sword kept ready for use in the scabbard of caution. It is your shield. Moral cowardice degrades one more than physical weakness. Many have had eminent qualities yet, for want of a stout heart, they passed inanimate lives and found a tomb in their own sloth. Wise nature has thoughtfully combined in the bee the sweetness of its honey with the sharpness of its sting.

· 55 ·

KNOW HOW TO WAIT. It is a sign of a noble heart to be endowed with patience, never to be in a hurry, never to be given over to passion. First be master over yourself if you would be master over others. You must pass through the circumference of time before arriving at the center of opportunity. A wise reserve seasons the aims and matures the means. Time's crutch effects more than the iron club of Hercules. God himself chastens not with a rod but with time. "Time and I against any two," is a great saying. Fortune rewards the first prize to those who wait.

· 56 ·

HAVE PRESENCE OF MIND. This is the child of a happy readiness of spirit. Owing to this vivacity and alertness there is no fear of danger of accident. Many reflect much only to go wrong in the end and others attain their aim without thinking about it beforehand. There are paradoxical characters who work best in an emergency. They are like monsters who succeed in all they do offhand, but fail in everything they think over. Something occurs to them at once or never—for them there is no court of appeal. Promptness wins applause because it proves remarkable capacity: subtlety of judgment, prudence in action.

· 57 ·

BE SLOW AND SURE. Things are done quickly enough if done well. If just quickly done they can be quickly undone. To last an eternity requires an eternity of preparation. Only excellence counts, only achievement endures. Profound intelligence is the only foundation for immortality. What is worth much costs much. The precious metals are the heaviest.

· 58 ·

ADAPT YOURSELF TO THOSE AROUND YOU. There is no need to show your ability before everyone. Employ no more force than is necessary. Let there be no unnecessary expenditure either of knowledge or of power. The skillful falconer only flies enough birds to serve for the chase. If there is too much display today there will be nothing to show tomorrow. Always have some novelty with which to dazzle. To show something fresh each day keeps expectation alive and conceals the limits of capacity.

· 59 ·

FINISH OFF WELL. In the house of fortune if you enter by the gate of pleasure you must leave by that of sorrow, and vice versa. You ought therefore to think of the finish, and attach more importance to a happy exit than to applause on entrance. It is the common lot of the unlucky to have a very fortunate beginning and a very tragic end. The important point is not the vulgar applause on entrance—that comes to nearly all— but the general feeling at exit. Few in life are felt to deserve an encore. Fortune rarely accompanies anyone to the door, and as warmly as she may welcome the coming, she is cold to the parting guest.

· 60 ·

HAVE SOUND JUDGMENT. Some are born wise and with this natural advantage enter upon their studies with half their journey to success already mastered. With age and experience their reason ripens, and thus they attain a sound judgment. They abhor everything whimsical as leading prudence astray, especially in matters of state, where certainty is so necessary, owing to the importance of the affairs involved. Such people deserve to stand at the helm of government either as navigators or helmsmen.

· 61 ·

EXCEL IN WHAT IS EXCELLENT. It is a great rarity among excellences. You cannot have a great person without something preeminent. Mediocrity never wins applause. Eminence in some distinguished post distinguishes one from the vulgar mob and ranks us with the exceptional. To be distinguished in a small post is to be great in little—the more comfort the less glory. To be excellent at great things is a royal characteristic—it excites admiration and wins goodwill.

· 62 ·

USE GOOD INSTRUMENTS. Some would have the subtlety of their wits proven by the poorness of their instruments. This is a dangerous satisfaction and deserves a fatal punishment. The excellence of a minister never diminished the greatness of his lord. All the glory of exploits reverts to the principal actor, also all the blame. Fame only does business with principals. She does not say, "This had good, that had bad servants," but, "This was a good artist, that a bad one." Therefore, let your assistants be selected and tested, for you have to trust to them an immortality of fame.

· 63 ·

TO BE THE FIRST OF THE KIND IS EXCELLENT. And to be eminent in it as well is twice as good. To have the first move is a great advantage when the players are equal. Many a person would have been as unique as a phoenix if he had been the first of the sort. Those who come first are the heirs of fame. The others get only a younger brother's allowance; whatever they do, they cannot persuade the world they are anything more than parrots. Extraordinary people find a new path to eminence, and prudence accompanies them all the way. Because of the novelty of their enterprises, sages write their names in the golden book of heroes. Some prefer to be first in things of minor importance than second in greater exploits.

· 64 ·

AVOID WORRY. Such prudence brings its own reward. It escapes much, and is thus the midwife of comfort and so of happiness. Neither give nor take bad news unless it can help. Some people's ears are stuffed with the sweets of flattery, others with the bitters of scandal, while some cannot live without a daily annoyance no more than Mithridates could without poison.* It is no rule of life to prepare for yourself lifelong trouble in order to give a temporary enjoyment to another, however near and dear. You should never spoil your own chances in order to please another who advises but keeps out of the affair. And if in order to please another you have to cause yourself pain, remember the rule that it is better that he should suffer now than you should suffer afterwards and in vain.

· 65 ·

CULTIVATE TASTE. You can train it like the intellect. Full knowledge whets desire and increases enjoyment. You may know a noble spirit by the elevation of his taste. Only a great thing can satisfy a great mind. Big bites for big mouths, lofty things for lofty spirits. Before their judgment the bravest tremble, the most perfect lose confidence. Few things are of the first importance, so let appreciation be rare. Taste can be imparted by personal intercourse; it is great good luck to associate with the highest taste. But do not profess to be dissatisfied with everything; this is the extreme of folly, and more odious if from affectation than if from unreachable ideals. Some would have God create another world and other ideals to satisfy their fantastic imagination.

· 66 ·

SEE TO IT THAT THINGS END WELL. Some regard more the rigor of the game than the winning of it, but to the world the discredit of the final

---

* Mithridates VI (132?–63 B.C.E.), King of Pontus, is said to have taken small doses of poison to immunize himself from it in the event that it might be used in an assassination attempt.—Ed.

failure does away with any recognition of previous diligence. The victor need not explain. The world does not notice the details of the measures employed, but only the good or bad result. You lose nothing if you gain your end. A good end gilds everything, however unsatisfactory the means. Thus at times it is part of the art of life to transgress the rules of the art, if you cannot end well otherwise.

· 67 ·

CHOOSE AN OCCUPATION THAT WINS DISTINCTION. Most things depend on the satisfaction of others. Esteem is to excellence what the west wind is to flowers: the breath of life. There are some occupations that gain universal esteem, while others more important are without credit. The former, pursued before the eyes of all, obtain the universal favor; the others, though they are rarer and more valuable, remain obscure and unperceived, honored but not applauded. Among princes, conquerors are the most celebrated, and therefore the kings of Aragon earned such applause as warriors, conquerors, and great people. An able person will prefer occupations of distinction, which all know of and utilize—he thus becomes immortalized by universal suffrage.

· 68 ·

IT IS BETTER TO HELP WITH INTELLIGENCE THAN WITH MEMORY. The latter needs only recollection, the former requires thought. Many people fail to do what is appropriate to the moment because it does not occur to them. A friend's advice on such occasions may enable them to see the advantages. It is one of the greatest gifts of mind to be able to offer what is needed at the right moment; for want of that many things fail to be performed. Share the light of your intelligence, when you have any, and ask for it when you have it not—the first cautiously, the last anxiously. Give no more than a hint. This finesse is especially necessary when it touches the interests of him whose attention you awaken. You should give but a taste at first, and then pass on more when that is not sufficient. If he thinks of *no,* go cleverly in search of *yes.* Most things are not obtained simply because they are not attempted.

· 69 ·

DO NOT GIVE WAY TO EVERY COMMON IMPULSE. He is great who never allows himself to be influenced by the impressions of others. Self-reflection is the school of wisdom; to know one's current disposition and to allow for it, even going to the other extreme so as to find a balance between nature and art. Self-knowledge is the beginning of self-improvement. There are some whose humors are so monstrous that they are always under the influence of one or other of them and put them in place of their real inclinations. They are torn asunder by such disharmony and get involved in contradictory obligations. Such excesses not only destroy firmness of will, all power of judgment gets lost and desire and knowledge pull in opposite directions.

· 70 ·

KNOW HOW TO SAY "NO." One ought not to give way in everything nor to everybody. To know how to refuse is therefore as important as to know how to consent. This is especially the case with people of power. Everything depends on how you do it. Some people's *no* is thought more of than the *yes* of others; for a gilded *no* is more satisfactory than a dry *yes.* There are some who always have *no* on their lips, whereby they make everything distasteful. *No* always comes first with them, and when sometimes they give way after all, it does them no good on account of the unpleasant beginning. Your refusal need not be point-blank; let the disappointment come by degrees. Nor let the refusal be final—that would destroy dependence, so let some spice of hope remain to soften the rejection. Let politeness compensate and fine words supply the place of deeds. *Yes* and *no* are soon said, but give much to think over.

· 71 ·

Do not vacillate. Do not let your actions be abnormal either from disposition or affectation. A wise person is always consistent in his best qualities, and because of this he gets the credit of trustworthiness. If he changes, he does so for good reason and after good consideration. In matters of conduct change is hateful. There are some who are different every day—their intelligence varies, still more their will, and with this their fortune. Yesterday's white is today's black; today's *no* was yesterday's *yes*. They always give the lie to their own credit and destroy their credit with others.

· 72 ·

Be resolute. Bad execution of your designs does less harm than irresolution in forming them. Streams do less harm flowing than when dammed up. There are some people so infirm of purpose that they always require direction from others, and this not on account of any perplexity, for they judge clearly, but from sheer incapacity for action. It takes some skill to find out difficulties but more to find a way out of them. There are others who never get bogged down; their clear judgment and determined character fit them for the highest callings, their intelligence tells them where to insert the thin end of the wedge, their resolution how to drive it home. They soon get through anything, and when they have done with one sphere of action, they are ready for another. Wedded to fortune, they make themselves sure of success.

· 73 ·

Know how to use evasion. That is how smart people get out of difficulties. They extricate themselves from the most intricate labyrinth by some witty application of a bright remark. They get out of a serious contention by an airy nothing or by raising a smile. Most of the great leaders are well grounded in this art. When you have to refuse something, often the most courteous way is to just change the subject. And sometimes it proves the highest understanding to act like you do not understand.

· 74 ·

DO NOT BE UNAPPROACHABLE. The most wild beasts live in the most populous places. To be inaccessible is the fault of those who distrust themselves, whose honors change their manners. It is no way to earn people's goodwill by being ill-tempered with them. What a sight it is to see one of those unsociable monsters who make a point of being proudly impertinent. Their servants, who have the misfortune to be obliged to speak with them, enter as if prepared for a fight with a tiger: armed with patience and with fear. To obtain their high position these unapproachable people must have ingratiated themselves with everyone, but having arrived there they seek to compensate themselves by irritating all. It is a condition of their position that they should be accessible to all, yet from pride or spite they are so to none. A civil way to punish such people is to let them alone, depriving them of the chance of improvement by granting them no opportunity for intercourse.

· 75 ·

CHOOSE A HEROIC IDEAL. Emulate rather than imitate. There are exemplars of greatness, living texts of honor. Let everyone have before his mind the best in his profession, not so much to follow him as to spur himself on. Alexander wept not on account of Achilles being dead and buried, but over himself because his fame had not yet spread throughout the world. Nothing arouses ambition so much in the heart as the trumpet call of another's fame. The same thing that sharpens envy nourishes a generous spirit.

· 76 ·

DO NOT ALWAYS BE JOKING. Wisdom is shown in serious matters, and is more appreciated than mere wit. He that is always ready for jests is never ready for serious things. Jokers resemble liars in that people never believe either, always expecting a lie in one, a joke in the other. One never knows when you speak with judgment, which is the same as if you had none. A continual jest soon loses all zest. Many get the reputation for being witty but thereby lose the credit of being sensible. Jest has its little hour, seriousness should have all the rest.

· 77 ·

BE ALL THINGS TO ALL PEOPLE. Be a discreet Proteus, learned with the learned, saintly with the sainted. It is the great art to gain everyone's support; general agreement gains goodwill. Notice people's moods and adapt yourself to each, genial or serious as the case may be. Follow their lead, glossing over the changes as cunningly as possible. This is an especially indispensable art for people who are dependent on others. But this skill in the art of living calls for great cleverness. He only will find no difficulty who has a universal genius in his knowledge and universal ingenuity in his wit.

· 78 ·

THE ART OF UNDERTAKING THINGS. Fools rush in through the door— for folly is always bold. The same simplicity that robs them of all attention to caution deprives them of all sense of shame at failure. But prudence enters with more deliberation. Its forerunners are caution and care; they advance and discover whether you can also advance without danger. Every rush forward might have been freed from danger by caution, but fortune sometimes helps in such cases. Go cautiously where you suspect depth. Sagacity goes cautiously forward while discretion covers the ground. Nowadays there are unsuspected depths in human intercourse, you must therefore plumb the waters as you go.

· 79 ·

A JOVIAL DISPOSITION. With moderation it is an accomplishment, not a defect. A grain of gaiety seasons all. The greatest people join in the fun at times and it makes them liked by all. But they should always on such occasions preserve their dignity nor go beyond the bounds of decorum. Others, again, use a joke to get themselves out of difficulty quickly. For there are things you must take in fun, though others perhaps mean them in earnest. This shows a sense of calm, which acts as a magnet on all hearts.

· 80 ·

TAKE CARE WHEN YOU GET INFORMATION. We live by information, not by sight. We exist by faith in others. The ear is the sidedoor of truth but the frontdoor of lies. The truth is generally seen, rarely heard. She seldom comes in elemental purity, especially from afar—there is always some admixture of the moods of those through whom she has passed. The passions tinge her with their colors wherever they touch her, sometimes favorably, sometimes odiously. She always brings out people's disposition, therefore receive her with caution from him that praises, with more caution from him that blames. Pay attention to the intention of the speaker; you should know beforehand on what footing he comes. Let reflection test for falsity and exaggeration.

· 81 ·

RENEW YOUR BRILLIANCE. This is the privilege of the phoenix. Ability grows old, and with it fame. The staleness of custom weakens admiration, and a mediocrity that is new often eclipses the highest excellence grown old. Try therefore to be born again in valor, in genius, in fortune, in everything. Display startling novelty—rise afresh like the sun every day. Change too the scene on which you shine, so that your loss may be felt in the old scenes of your triumph, while the novelty of your powers wins you applause in the new.

· 82 ·

DRAIN NOTHING TO THE DREGS, NEITHER GOOD NOR BAD. A sage once reduced all virtue to the golden mean. Push right to the extreme and it becomes wrong; press all the juice from an orange and it becomes bitter. Even in enjoyment never go to extremes. Thought too subtle is dull. If you milk a cow too much you draw blood, not milk.

· 83 ·

ALLOW YOURSELF SOME FORGIVABLE SIN. Some such carelessness is often the greatest recommendation of talent. For envy causes ostracism, most envenomed when most polite. Envy counts every perfection as a failing and that it has no faults itself. Being perfect in all envy condemns perfection in all. It becomes an Argus, all eyes for imperfection, if only for its own consolation.* Blame is like the lightning—it hits the highest. Let Homer nod now and then and affect some negligence in valor or in intellect—not in prudence—so as to disarm malevolence, or at least to prevent its bursting with its own venom. You thus leave your cape on the horns of envy in order to save your immortality.†

---

* In classical mythology, Argus was a giant with a hundred eyes.—Ed.
† Gracián takes this image from the technique of the matador, who holds the red cape to the side and allows the bull to charge.—Ed.

· 84 ·

MAKE USE OF YOUR ENEMIES. You should learn to seize things not by the blade, which cuts, but by the handle, which saves you from harm—especially with the doings of your enemies. A wise person gets more use from his enemies than a fool from his friends. Their ill will often levels mountains of difficulties that one would otherwise not face. Many have had their greatness made for them by their enemies. Flattery is more dangerous than hatred, because it covers the stains that the other causes to be wiped out. The wise will turn ill will into a mirror more faithful than that of kindness, and remove or improve the faults referred to. Caution thrives well when rivalry and ill will are next-door neighbors.

· 85 ·

DO NOT BE A WILD CARD, A JACK-OF-ALL-TRADES. It is a fault of excellence that being so much in use it is liable to abuse. Because all covet it, all are vexed by it. It is great misfortune to be of use to nobody—scarcely less to be of use to everybody. People who reach this stage lose by gaining, and in the end bore those who desired them before. These wild cards wear away all kinds of excellence. Losing the earlier esteem of the few, they obtain discredit among the vulgar. The remedy against this extreme is to moderate your brilliance. Be extraordinary in your excellence, if you like, but be ordinary in your display of it. The more light a torch gives, the more it burns away and the nearer it is to burning out. Show yourself less and you will be rewarded by being esteemed more.

· 86 ·

PREVENT SCANDAL. Many heads go to make the mob, and in each of them there are eyes for malice to use and a tongue for detraction to wag. If a single ill report spreads, it casts a blemish on your fair fame, and if it clings to you with a nickname, your reputation is in danger. Generally it is some salient defect or ridiculous trait that gives rise to the rumors. At times these are malicious inflations of private envy to general distrust. For these are wicked tongues that ruin a great reputation more easily by a witty sneer than by a direct accusation. It is easy to get a bad reputation because it is easy to believe evil but hard to eradicate. The wise therefore avoid such incidents, guarding against vulgar scandal with constant vigilance. It is far easier to prevent than to rectify.

· 87 ·

CULTURE AND ELEGANCE. We are born barbarians and only raise ourselves above the beast by culture. Culture therefore makes the person; the greater a person the more culture. Thanks to this, Greece could call the rest of the world barbarians. Ignorance is very raw—nothing contributes so much to culture as knowledge. But even knowledge is coarse if without elegance. Not alone must our intelligence be elegant, but also our desires, and above all our conversation. Some people are naturally elegant in internal and external qualities, in their thoughts, in their words, in their dress, which is the rind of the soul as their talents are its fruit. There are others, on the other hand, so gauche that everything about them, even their most excellent quality, is tarnished by an intolerable and barbaric want of neatness.

· 88 ·

LET YOUR BEHAVIOR BE FINE AND NOBLE. A great person ought not to be little in his actions. He ought never to pry too minutely into things, least of all in unpleasant matters. For though it is important to know all, it is not necessary to know all about all. One ought to act in such cases with the generosity of a gentleman, with conduct worthy of a gallant person. To pretend to overlook things is a large part of the work of ruling. Most things must be left unnoticed among relatives and friends, and even among enemies. All superfluity is annoying, especially in things that annoy. To keep hovering around the object of your annoyance is a kind of mania. Generally speaking, everybody behaves according to his heart and his understanding.

· 89 ·

KNOW YOURSELF. Know your talents and capacity, in judgment and inclination. You cannot master yourself unless you know yourself. There are mirrors for the face but none for the mind. Let careful thought about yourself serve as a substitute. When the outer image is forgotten, keep the inner one to improve and perfect. Learn the force of your intellect and capacity for affairs, test the force of your courage in order to apply it, and keep your foundations secure and your head clear for everything.

· 90 ·

THE SECRET OF LONG LIFE. Lead a good life. Two things bring life speedily to an end: folly and immorality. Some lose their life because they have not the intelligence to keep it, others because they have not the will. Just as virtue is its own reward, so is vice its own punishment. He who lives a fast life runs through life to its end doubly quick. A virtuous life never dies. The firmness of the soul is communicated to the body, and a good life is not only long but also full.

· 91 ·

NEVER SET TO WORK AT ANYTHING IF YOU HAVE ANY DOUBTS ABOUT ITS PRUDENCE. A suspicion of failure in the mind of the doer is proof positive of it in that of the onlooker, especially if he is a rival. If in the heat of action your judgment wavers, it will afterwards in cool reflection be condemned as folly. Action is dangerous where prudence is in doubt—better leave such things alone. Wisdom does not trust to probabilities, it always marches in the midday light of reason. How can an enterprise succeed which the judgment condemns as soon as it was conceived? If resolutions passed unanimously by an inner court often turn out badly, what can we expect of those undertaken by a doubting reason and a vacillating judgment?

· 92 ·

TRANSCENDENT WISDOM. I mean in everything. An ounce of wisdom is worth more than a ton of cleverness is the first and highest rule of all deeds and words, the more necessary to be followed the higher and more numerous your post. It is the only sure way, though it may not gain so much applause. A reputation for wisdom is the last triumph of fame. It is enough if you satisfy the wise, for their judgment is the touchstone of true success.

· 93 ·

VERSATILITY. A man of many excellent qualities equals many men. By imparting his own enjoyment of life to his circle of friends and followers he enriches their life. Variety in excellences is the delight of life. It is a great art to profit by all that is good, and, since nature has made people in their most perfected form an abstract of herself, so let art create in them a true microcosm by training their taste and intellect.

· 94 ·

KEEP THE EXTENT OF YOUR ABILITIES UNKNOWN. The wise person does not allow his knowledge and abilities to be sounded to the bottom, if he desires to be honored by all. He allows you to know him but not to comprehend him. No one must know the extent of a wise person's abilities, lest he be disappointed. No one should ever have an opportunity to fathom him entirely. For guesses and doubts about the extent of his talents arouse more veneration than accurate knowledge of them, be they ever so great.

· 95 ·

KEEP EXPECTATION ALIVE. Keep stirring it up. Let much promise more, and great deeds herald greater. Do not rest your whole fortune on a single cast of the dice. It requires great skill to moderate your forces so as to keep expectation from being dissipated.

· 96 ·

THE HIGHEST DISCRETION. It is the throne of reason, the foundation of prudence—by its means success is gained at little cost. It is a gift from above, and should be prayed for as the first and best quality. It is the main piece of the suit of armor, and so important that its absence makes a person imperfect, whereas with other qualities it is merely a question of needing more or less. All the actions of life depend on its application—all require its assistance, for everything needs intelligence. Discretion consists in a natural tendency to the most rational course, combined with a liking for the surest.

· 97 ·

OBTAIN AND PRESERVE A REPUTATION. It is something only borrowed from fame. It is expensive to obtain a reputation, for it only attaches to distinguished abilities, which are as rare as mediocrities are common. Once obtained, it is easily preserved. It confers many an obligation, but it does more. When it is owing to elevated powers or lofty spheres of action, it rises to a kind of veneration and yields a sort of majesty. But it is only a well-founded reputation that lasts permanently.

· 98 ·

WRITE YOUR INTENTIONS IN CYPHER. The passions are the gates of the soul. The most practical knowledge consists in disguising them. He that plays with cards exposed runs a risk of losing the stakes. The reserve of caution should combat the curiosity of inquirers with the policy of the inky cuttlefish. Do not even let your tastes be known, lest others utilize them either by running counter to them or by flattering them.

· 99 ·

REALITY AND APPEARANCE. Things pass for what they seem, not for what they are. Few see inside, many get attached to appearances. It is not enough to be right if your actions look false and ill.

· 100 ·

BE A PERSON WITHOUT ILLUSIONS, ONE WHO IS WISE AND RIGH-TEOUS, A PHILOSOPHICAL COURTIER. Be all these, not merely seem to be them, still less affect to be them. Philosophy is nowadays discred-ited, but yet it was always the chief concern of the wise. The art of thinking has been degraded. Seneca introduced it at Rome, it found favor for a time among nobility, but now it is considered nonsense. And yet the discovery of deceit was always thought the true nourishment of a thoughtful mind, the true delight of a virtuous soul.

· 101 ·

ONE HALF OF THE WORLD LAUGHS AT THE OTHER, AND FOOLS ARE THEY ALL. Everything is good or everything is bad according to who you ask. What one pursues another persecutes. He is an insufferable ass who would regulate everything according to his ideas. Excellences do not depend on a single person's pleasure. So many people, so many tastes, all different. There is no defect that is not affected by some. We need not lose heart if something does not please someone, for others will appreciate it; nor need their applause turn our head, for there will surely be others to condemn it. The real test of praise is the approval of renowned people and of experts in the field. You should aim to be independent of any one opinion, of any one fashion, of any one century.

· 102 ·

BE ABLE TO STOMACH BIG SLICES OF LUCK. In the body of wisdom not the least important organ is a big stomach, for great capacity implies great parts. Big bits of luck do not embarrass one who can digest still bigger ones. What is a surfeit for one may be hunger for another. Many are troubled as it were with weak digestion, owing to their small capacity, being neither born nor trained for great employment. Their actions turn sour, and the fumes that arise from their undeserved honors turn their head and make them dizzy—a great risk in high positions. They do not find their proper place, for luck finds no proper place in them. A person of talent therefore should show that he has more room for even greater enterprises, and above all avoid showing signs of a little heart.

· 103 ·

LET EACH KEEP UP HIS DIGNITY. Let each deed of a person in its degree, though he be not a king, be worthy of a prince and let his action be princely within due limits. Sublime in action, lofty in thought, in all things like a king, at least in merit if not in might. For true kingship lies in spotless rectitude, and he need not envy greatness who can serve as a model of it. Especially should those near the throne aim at true superiority, and prefer to share the true qualities of royalty rather than take parts in its mere ceremonies—yet without affecting its imperfections but sharing in its true dignity.

· 104 ·

GET TO KNOW WHAT IS NEEDED IN DIFFERENT OCCUPATIONS. Different qualities are required. To know which is needed taxes attention and calls for masterly discernment. Some demand courage, others tact. Those that merely require rectitude are the easiest, the most difficult are those requiring cleverness. For the former all that is necessary is character, for the latter all of one's attention and zeal may not suffice. It is a troublesome business to rule people, still more fools or blockheads—twice as much sense is needed with those who have none. It is intolerable when an office engrosses someone with fixed hours and a settled routine. Those are better that leave him free to follow his own devices, combining variety with importance, for the change refreshes the mind. The most respected jobs are those that have least, or most distant, dependence on others. The worst are those that worry us both here and hereafter.

· 105 ·

DO NOT BE A BORE. The person obsessed with one activity or one topic is apt to be tiresome. Brevity is flattering and gets more accomplished—it gains by courtesy what it loses by curtness. Good things, when short, are twice as good. The quintessence of the matter is more effective than a big mishmash of details. It is a well-known truth that a talkative person rarely is wise, whether in dealing with things at hand or how they function. There are people who serve more as stumbling blocks than centerpieces, useless lumber in everyone's way. The wise avoid being bores, especially to the great—who are fully occupied; it is worse to disturb one of them than all the rest. Well said is soon said.

· 106 ·

DO NOT PARADE YOUR POSITION. To boast about your position is more offensive than personal vanity. To pose as an important person is to be hated—you should surely have had enough of envy. The more you seek esteem the less you obtain it, for it depends on the opinion of others. You cannot take it, but must earn and receive it from others. Great positions require exercising a sufficient amount of authority—without it they cannot be adequately filled. Preserve therefore enough dignity to carry on the duties of the office. Do not enforce respect, but try to create it. Those who insist on the dignity of their office, show they have not deserved it, and that it is too much for them. If you wish to be valued, be valued for your talents, not for anything obtained by chance. Even kings prefer to be honored for their personal qualifications rather than for their station.

· 107 ·

SHOW NO SELF-SATISFACTION. You must neither be discontented with yourself, which is weak-spirited, nor self-satisfied, which is folly. Self-satisfaction arises mostly from ignorance, and it would be a happy ignorance not without its advantages if it did not ruin reputation. Because a person cannot achieve the superlative perfections of others, he contents himself with any mediocre talent of his own. Distrust is wise, and even useful, either to evade mishaps or to afford consolation when they come, for a misfortune cannot surprise a man who has already feared it. Even Homer nods at times, and Alexander fell from his lofty state due to his illusions. Things depend on many circumstances—what constitutes triumph in one set may cause a defeat in another. In the midst of all, incorrigible folly remains the same with empty self-satisfaction, blossoming, flowering, and running all to seed.

· 108 ·

THE SHORTEST PATH TO GREATNESS IS ALONG WITH OTHERS. Intercourse with the right people works well; manners and taste are shared, good sense and even talent grow insensibly. Let the impatient person then make a comrade of the sluggish, and so with the other temperaments, so that without forcing it the golden mean is obtained. It is a great art to agree with others. The alternation of contraries beautifies and sustains the world, and if it can cause harmony in the physical world, still more can it do so in the moral. Adopt this policy in the choice of friends and defendants—by joining extremes the more effective middle way is found.

· 109 ·

DO NOT BE CENSORIOUS. There are people of gloomy character who regard everything as faulty, not from any evil motive but because it is their nature to. They condemn all—these for what they have done, those for what they will do. This indicates a nature worse than cruel, vile indeed. They accuse with such exaggeration that they make out of motes beams with which to poke out the eyes. They are always taskmasters who could turn a paradise into a prison—if passion intervenes they drive matters to the extreme. A noble nature, on the contrary, always knows how to find an excuse for failings, saying the intention was good, or it was only an error of oversight.

· 110 ·

DO NOT WAIT TILL YOU ARE A SETTING SUN. It is a maxim of the wise to leave things before things leave them. One should be able to snatch a triumph at the end, just as the sun even at its brightest often retires behind a cloud so as not to be seen sinking, and to leave in doubt whether he has sunk or not. Wisely withdraw from the mere chance of mishap, lest you have to do so when it becomes reality. Do not wait until they turn you the cold shoulder and carry you to the grave, alive in feeling but dead in esteem. Wise trainers put racehorses out to pasture before they arouse derision by falling on the course. A beauty should break her mirror early, lest she do so later with open eyes.

· 111 ·

HAVE FRIENDS. A friend is a second self. Every friend is good and wise for his friend; between them everything turns to good. Everyone is as others wish him to be—but in order that they may wish him well, he must win their hearts and so their tongues. There is no magic like a good turn, and the way to gain friendly feelings is to do friendly acts. The most and best of us depend on others—we have to live either among friends or among enemies. So seek someone everyday who will wish you well—if not a friend, by-and-by after trials some of these will become your confidants.

· 112 ·

GAIN GOODWILL. For thus the first and highest cause foresees and furthers the greatest objects. By gaining their goodwill you gain people's good opinion. Some trust so much to merit that they neglect grace, but wise men know that it is a long and stony road without a lift from favor. Goodwill facilitates and supplies everything. It supposes gifts or even supplies them, such as courage, zeal, knowledge, or even discretion; whereas it will not see defects because it does not search for them. It arises from some common interest, either material, as in disposition, nationality, family, race, occupation; or formal, which is of a higher kind of communion, as in capacity, obligation, reputation, or merit. The whole difficulty is to gain goodwill—to keep it is easy. It has, however, to be sought for and when found to be utilized.

· 113 ·

IN TIMES OF PROSPERITY PREPARE FOR ADVERSITY. It is both wiser and easier to collect winter stores in summer. In prosperity favors are cheap and friends are many. It is well therefore to save them for more unlucky days, for adversity costs dear and has no helpers. Retain a store of friends and people who are in your debt—the day may come when their price will go up. Lowly minds never have friends—in luck they will not recognize them, in misfortune they will not be recognized by them.

· 114 ·

NEVER COMPETE. Every competition damages your reputation. Our rivals seize occasion to obscure us so as to outshine us. Few wage honorable war. Rivalry discloses faults that courtesy would hide. Many have lived in good repute while they had no rivals. The heat of conflict revives and gives new life to dead scandals, digging up long-buried skeletons. Competition begins with belittling, and seeks aid anywhere it can, not only where it should. And when the weapons of abuse do not effect their purpose, as often or mostly happens, our opponents seek revenge and use them at least for beating away the dust of oblivion from anything that is our discredit. People of goodwill are always at peace, and those of good reputation and dignity are of goodwill.

· 115 ·

GET USED TO THE FAILINGS OF THOSE AROUND YOU. Just as you would to an ugly face. It is indispensable if they depend on you, or you on them. There are wretched characters one cannot live with or without. Therefore clever folk get used to them, as to ugly faces, so that they are not obliged to do so suddenly under the pressure of necessity. At first they arouse disgust, but gradually they lose this influence, and reflection provides for disgust or puts up with it.

· 116 ·

ONLY ACT WITH HONORABLE PEOPLE. You can trust them and they you. Their honor is the best surety of their behavior even in misunderstandings, for they always act according to their character. Hence it is better to have a dispute with honorable people than to have a victory over dishonorable ones. You cannot deal well with the ruined, for they have no hostages for rectitude. With them there is no true friendship, and their agreements are not binding, however stringent they may appear, because they have no feeling of honor. Never have anything to do with such people, for if honor does not restrain them, virtue will not, since honor is the throne of rectitude.

· 117 ·

NEVER TALK ABOUT YOURSELF. To do so you must either praise yourself, which is vain, or blame yourself, which is weak-minded—it is unseemly for the speaker and unpleasant for the listener. And if you should avoid this in ordinary conversation, how much more so in official matters, and above all in public speaking, where every mere appearance of unwisdom really is unwise. The same want of tact lies in speaking of someone in his presence, owing to the danger of going to one of two extremes: flattery or censure.

· 118 ·

ACQUIRE THE REPUTATION FOR COURTESY. This is enough to make you liked. Politeness is the main ingredient of culture—a kind of witchery that wins the regard of all as surely as discourtesy gains their disfavor and opposition. If this latter springs from pride it is abominable, if from bad breeding it is despicable. Better too much courtesy than too little, provided it is not indiscriminate, which degenerates into injustice. Between opponents it is of special worth as a proof of valor. It costs little and helps much—everyone is honored who gives honor. Politeness and honor have this advantage, that they remain with him who displays them to others.

· 119 ·

AVOID BECOMING DISLIKED. There is no right occasion to seek dislike—it comes without seeking soon enough. There are many who hate of their own accord without knowing the why or the how. Their ill will outruns our readiness to please. Their ill nature is more prone to do harm to others than their greed is eager to gain advantage for themselves. Some manage to be on bad terms with everyone because they always either produce or experience vexation of spirit. Once hate has taken root it is, like bad reputation, difficult to eradicate. Wise people are feared, the malevolent are abhorred, the arrogant are regarded with disdain, buffoons with contempt, eccentrics with neglect. Therefore pay respect that you may be respected, and know that to be esteemed you must show esteem.

· 120 ·

LIVE PRACTICALLY. Even knowledge has to be in style, and where it is not it is wise to affect ignorance. Thought and taste change with the times. Do not be old-fashioned in your ways of thinking and let your taste be modern. In everything the taste of the many carries the day; for the time being one must follow it in the hope of leading it to higher things. In the adornment of the body, as of the mind, adapt yourself to the present, even though the past appears better. But this rule does not apply to kindness, for goodness is for all times. It is neglected nowadays and seems out of date. Truthfulness, keeping your word, and so too good people, seem to come from the good old days, yet they are liked for all that, but even so if any exist they are not in fashion and are not imitated. What a misfortune for our age that it regards virtue as a stranger and vice as a matter of course! If you are wise live as you can, if you cannot live as you would. Think more highly of what fate has given you than of what it has denied.

· 121 ·

DO NOT MAKE MUCH ADO ABOUT NOTHING. As some make gossip out of everything, so others make much ado of everything. They always talk big, take everything in earnest and turn it into a dispute or a secret. Troublesome things must not be taken too seriously if they can be avoided. It is preposterous to take to heart that which you should just throw over your shoulders. Much that would be something has become nothing by being left alone, and what was nothing has become of consequence by being made much of. At the outset things can be easily settled, but not afterwards. Often the remedy causes the disease. It is by no means the least of life's rules to let things alone.

· 122 ·

DISTINCTION IN SPEECH AND ACTION. By this you gain a position in many places and win esteem in advance. It shows itself in everything, in talk, in look, even in gait. It is a great victory to conquer people's hearts. It does not arise from any foolish presumption or pompous talk, but in a becoming tone of authority born of superior talent combined with true merit.

· 123 ·

AVOID AFFECTATION. The more merit, the less affectation, which gives a vulgar flavor to all. It is wearisome to others and troublesome to the one affected, for he becomes a martyr to care and tortures himself with attention. The most eminent merits lose most by it, for they appear proud and artificial instead of being the product of nature, and the natural is always more pleasing than the artificial. One always feels sure that the person who affects a virtue has it not. The more pains you take with a thing, the more you should conceal them, so that it may appear to arise spontaneously from your own natural character. Do not, however, in avoiding affectation fall into it by affecting to be unaffected. The sage never seems to know his own merits, for only by not noticing them can you call others' attention to them. He is twice great who has all the perfections in the opinion of all except of himself—he attains applause by two opposite paths.

· 124 ·

MAKE YOURSELF SOUGHT AFTER. Few reach such favor with the many, if with the wise it is the height of happiness. When one has finished one's work, coldness is the general rule. But there are ways of earning the reward of goodwill. The sure way is to excel in your office and talents; add to this agreeable manner and you reach the point where you become necessary to your office, not your office to you. Some do honor to their post, with others it is the other way around. It is no great gain if a poor successor makes the predecessor seem good, for this does not imply that the one is missed, but that the other is wished away.

· 125 ·

DO NOT BE A BLACKLISTER OF OTHER PEOPLE'S FAULTS. It is a sign of having a tarnished name to concern oneself with the ill fame of others. Some wish to hide their own stains with those of others, or at least wash them away; or they seek consolation therein—it is the consolation of fools. Their breath must stink who form the sewers of scandal for the whole town. The more one grubs about in such matters the more one befouls oneself. There are few without stain somewhere or other. It is only of little known people that the failings are little known. Be careful then to avoid being a registrar of faults. That is to be an abominable thing, a man that lives without a heart.

· 126 ·

FOLLY CONSISTS NOT IN COMMITTING FOLLY, BUT IN NOT HIDING IT WHEN COMMITTED. You should keep your desires sealed up, still more your defects. All go wrong sometimes, but the wise try to hide their errors while fools boast of them. Reputation depends more on what is hidden than on what is done; if a man does not live chastely, he must live cautiously. The errors of great men are like the eclipses of the greater lights. Even in friendship it is rare to expose one's failings to one's friend. Nay, one should conceal them from oneself if one can. But here one can help with that other great rule of life: learn to forget.

· 127 ·

GRACE IN EVERYTHING. It is the life of talent, the breath of speech, the soul of action, and the ornament of ornament. Perfections are the adornment of our nature, but this is the adornment of perfection itself. It shows itself even in the thoughts. It is mostly a gift of nature and owes least to education—it even triumphs over training. It is more than ease, approaches the free and easy, gets over embarrassment, and adds the finishing touch to perfection. Without it beauty is lifeless, graciousness ungraceful. It surpasses valor, discretion, prudence, even majesty itself. It is a shortcut to accomplishment and an easy escape from embarrassment.

· 128 ·

HIGHMINDEDNESS. This is one of the principal qualifications for a gentleman, it spurs us on to all kinds of nobility. It improves the taste, ennobles the heart, elevates the mind, refines the feelings, and intensifies dignity. It raises him in whom it is found. At times it even remedies the bad turns of fortune, which turns itself around because of envy. Highmindedness can find full scope in the will when it cannot be exercised in act. Magnanimity, generosity, and all heroic qualities recognize in it their source.

· 129 ·

NEVER COMPLAIN. To complain always brings discredit. Better to be a model of self-reliance opposed to the passion of others than an object of their compassion. For complaining opens the way for the hearer to act like those we are complaining of, and to disclose one insult forms an excuse for another. By complaining of past offenses we give occasion for future ones, and in seeking aid or counsel we only obtain indifference or contempt. It is much more politic to praise a person's favors, so that others may feel obliged to follow suit. To recount the favors we owe the absent is to demand similar ones from those present, and thus we sell our credit with the one to the other. The shrewd will therefore never publish to the world his failures or his defects, but only those marks of consideration that serve to keep friendship alive and enmity silent.

· 130 ·

DO AND BE SEEN DOING. Things do not pass for what they are but for what they seem. To be of use and to know how to show it, is to be twice as useful. What is not seen is as if it was not. Even the right does not receive proper consideration if it does not seem right. The observant are far fewer in number than those who are deceived by appearances. Deceit rules—things are judged by their jackets and many things are other than they seem. But a good exterior is the best recommendation of the inner perfection.

· 131 ·

NOBILITY OF FEELING. There is a certain distinction of the soul, a highmindedness prompting to gallant acts, that gives an air of grace to the whole character. It is not found often, for it presupposes great magnanimity. Its chief characteristic is to speak well of an enemy and to act even better toward him. It shines brightest when a chance comes for revenge; not alone does it let the occasion pass but improves it by using a complete victory in order to display unexpected generosity. It is a fine stroke of policy—no, the very acme of statecraft. It makes no pretense to victory, for it pretends to nothing, and while obtaining its deserts it conceals its merits.

· 132 ·

REVISE YOUR JUDGMENTS. To appeal to an inner court of revision makes things safe. Especially when the course of action is not clear, you gain time either to confirm or improve your decision. It affords new grounds for strengthening or corroborating your judgment. And if it is a matter of giving, the gift is the more valued from its being evidently well considered than for being too promptly bestowed; long expected is highest prized. And if you have to deny something, that gains you time to decide how and when to mature the *no* so that it may be made palatable. Besides, after the first heat of desire is passed the repulse of refusal is felt less keenly. But, especially when people press for a reply, it is best to defer it, for as often as not that is only a feint to disarm attention.

· 133 ·

BETTER MAD WITH THE REST OF THE WORLD THAN WISE ALONE. So say politicians. If all are so, one is no worse off than the rest, whereas solitary wisdom passes for folly. So important is it to sail with the stream. The greatest wisdom often consists in ignorance, or the pretense of it. One has to live with others, and others are mostly ignorant. "To live entirely alone one must be very like a god or quite like a wild beast," but I would turn the aphorism by saying: Better be wise with the many than a fool all alone. There be some too who seek to be original by chasing chimeras.

· 134 ·

DOUBLE YOUR RESOURCES. You thereby double your life. One must not depend on one thing or trust to only one resource, however preeminent. Everything should be kept double, especially the causes of success, of favor, or of esteem. The moon's mutability transcends everything and gives a limit to all existence, especially of things dependent on human will—the most brittle of all things. To guard against this inconstancy should be the sage's care, and for this the chief rule of life is to keep a double store of good and useful qualities. Thus as nature gives us in duplicate the most important of our limbs and those most exposed to risk, so art should deal with the qualities on which we depend for success.

· 135 ·

DO NOT NOURISH THE SPIRIT OF CONTRADICTION. It only proves you foolish or peevish and prudence should guard against this strenuously. To find difficulties in everything may prove you clever but such wrangling writes you down as a fool. Such folk make a war out of the most pleasant conversation and in this way act as enemies toward their associates rather than toward those with whom they do not consort. Grit grates most in delicacies, and so does contradiction in amusement. They are both foolish and cruel who yoke together the wild beast and the tame.

· 136 ·

POST YOURSELF IN THE CENTER OF THINGS. So you feel the pulse of affairs. Many lose their way either in the ramifications of useless discussion or in the brushwood of wearisome verbosity without ever realizing the real matter at hand. They go over a single point a hundred times, wearying themselves and others, and yet never touch the all important center of affairs. This comes from a confusion of mind from which they cannot extricate themselves. They waste time and patience on matters they should leave alone, and afterward there is no time spared for what they have left alone.

· 137 ·

THE SAGE SHOULD BE SELF-SUFFICIENT. He that was all in all to himself carried all with him when he carried himself. If a universal friend can represent to us Rome and the rest of the world, let a man be his own universal friend, and then he is in a position to live alone. Whom could such a man want if there is no clearer intellect or finer taste than his own? He would then depend on himself alone, which is the highest happiness and like the Supreme Being. He that can live alone resembles the brute beast in nothing, the sage in much and like a god in everything.

· 138 ·

THE ART OF LETTING THINGS ALONE. The more so the wilder the waves of public or of private life. There are hurricanes in human affairs, tempests of passion, when it is wise to retire to a harbor and ride it out at anchor. Remedies often make diseases worse; in such cases one has to leave them to their natural course and the moral influence of time. It takes a wise doctor to know when not to prescribe, and at times the greater skill consists in not applying remedies. The proper way to still the storms of the vulgar is to hold yourself back and let them calm down by themselves. To give way now is to conquer by and by. A fountain gets muddy with but little stirring up, and does not get clear by our meddling with it but by our leaving it alone. The best remedy for disturbances is to let them run their course, for so they quiet down.

· 139 ·

RECOGNIZE UNLUCKY DAYS. They do exist. Nothing goes well on them, and even though the game may be changed the bad luck remains. Two tries should be enough to tell if one is in luck today or not. Everything is in process of change, even the mind, and no one is always wise. Chance has something to say, even how to write a good letter. All perfection turns on the times—even beauty has its hours. Even wisdom fails at times by doing too much or too little. To turn out well a thing must be done on its own day. This is why with some people everything turns out ill, with others all goes well, even with less trouble. They find everything ready, their wit prompt, their presiding genius favorable, their lucky star on the rise. At such times one must seize the occasion and not throw away the slightest chance. But a shrewd person will not decide on the day's luck by a single piece of good or bad fortune, for the one may be only a lucky chance and the other only a slight annoyance.

· 140 ·

FIND THE GOOD IN A THING AT ONCE. This is the advantage of good taste. The bee goes to the honey for her comb, the serpent to the gall for its venom. So with taste—some seek the good, others the ill. There is nothing that has no good in it, especially in books, as giving food for thought. But many have such a scent that amid a thousand excellences they fix upon a single defect, and single it out for blame as if they were scavengers of people's hearts and minds. So they draw up a balance sheet of defects, which does more credit to their bad taste than to their intelligence. They lead a sad life, nourishing themselves on bitters and fattening on garbage. They have the luckier taste who amid a thousand defects seize upon a single beauty they may have hit upon by chance.

· 141 ·

DO NOT LISTEN TO YOURSELF. It is no use pleasing yourself if you do not please others, and as a rule general contempt is the punishment for self-satisfaction. The attention you pay to yourself you probably owe to others. To speak and at the same time listen to yourself cannot turn out well. If to talk to oneself when alone is madness, it must be doubly unwise to listen to oneself in the presence of others. It is a weakness of the great to talk with a recurrent "As I was saying" and "What?," which bewilders their hearers. At every sentence they look for applause or flattery, taxing the patience of the wise. So too the pompous speak with an echo, and as their talk can only totter on with the aid of stilts—at every word they need the support of a stupid "Bravo!"

· 142 ·

NEVER FROM OBSTINACY TAKE THE WRONG SIDE BECAUSE YOUR OP-PONENT HAS ANTICIPATED YOU BY TAKING THE RIGHT ONE. You begin the fight already beaten and must soon take to flight in disgrace. With bad weapons one can never win. It was astute in the opponent to seize the better side first, it would be folly to come lagging after with the worst. Such obstinacy is more dangerous in actions than in words, for action encounters more risk than talk. It is the common failing of the obstinate that they lose the true by contradicting it, and the useful by quarreling with it. The sage never places himself on the side of passion, but espouses the cause of right, either discovering it first or improving it later. If the enemy is a fool, he will in such a case turn round to follow the opposite and worse way. Thus the only way to drive him from the better course is to take it yourself, for his folly will cause him to desert it, and his obstinacy be punished for so doing.

· 143 ·

NEVER BECOME PARADOXICAL IN ORDER TO AVOID BEING TRITE. Both extremes damage our reputation. Every undertaking that differs from the reasonable approaches foolishness. The paradox is a cheat; it wins applause at first by its novelty and piquancy, but afterwards it becomes discredited when the deceit is foreseen and its emptiness becomes apparent. It is a species of jugglery, and in political matters it would be the ruin of the state. Those who cannot or dare not reach great deeds on the direct road of excellence go round by way of paradox, admired by fools but making wise men true prophets. It demonstrates an unbalanced judgment, and if it is not altogether based on the false, it is certainly founded on the uncertain, and risks the weightier matters of life.

· 144 ·

BEGIN WITH ANOTHER'S TO END WITH YOUR OWN. This is a politic means to your end. Even in heavenly matters Christian teachers lay stress on this holy cunning. It is a weighty piece of dissimulation, for the foreseen advantages serve as a lure to influence the other's will. His affair seems to be in train when it is really only leading the way for your own. One should never advance unless under cover, especially where the ground is dangerous. Likewise with persons who always say *no* at first, it is useful to ward off this blow by presenting your intent in such a way that the difficulty of conceding does not occur to them. This advice belongs to the rule about second thoughts [see maxim 13], which covers the most subtle maneuvers of life.

· 145 ·

DO NOT SHOW YOUR WOUNDED FINGER, FOR EVERYTHING WILL KNOCK UP AGAINST IT. Do not complain about it, for malice always aims where weakness can be injured. It is no use to be vexed; being the butt of the talk will only vex you the more. Ill will searches for wounds to irritate, aims darts to try the temper, and tries a thousand ways to sting to the quick. The wise never confess to being hit, or disclose any evil, whether personal or hereditary. For even fate sometimes likes to wound us where we are most tender. It always mortifies wounded flesh. Never therefore disclose the source of pain or of joy, if you wish the one to cease and the other to endure.

· 146 ·

LOOK INTO THE INTERIOR OF THINGS. Things are generally other than they seem, and ignorance that never looks beneath the rind is disillusioned when you show the kernel. Lies always come first, dragging fools along by their irreparable vulgarity. Truth always lags last, limping along on the arm of time. The wise therefore reserve for truth one of their ears, which their common mother, nature, has wisely given in duplicate. Deceit is very superficial, and the superficial therefore easily fall into it. Prudence lives retired within its recesses, visited only by sages and wise men.

· 147 ·

DO NOT BE INACCESSIBLE. None is so perfect that he does not need at times the advice of others. He is an incorrigible ass who will never listen to anyone. Even the most surpassing intellect should find a place for friendly counsel. Sovereignty itself must learn to lean. There are some that are incorrigible simply because they are inaccessible. They fall to ruin because none dares to extricate them. The highest should have the door open for friendship; it may prove the gate of help. A friend must be free to advise, and even to upbraid, without feeling embarrassed. Our satisfaction in him and our trust in his steadfast faith give him that power. One need not pay respect or give credit to everyone, but in the innermost sanctum of his caution a person must have the true mirror of a confidant to whom he owes the correction of his errors, and has to thank for it.

· 148 ·

HAVE THE ART OF CONVERSATION. That is where the real personality shows itself. No act requires more attention, though it be the most common thing in life. You must either lose or gain by it. If it takes care to write a letter, which is but a deliberate and written conversation, how much more so the ordinary kind in which there is occasion for a prompt display of intelligence? Experts feel the pulse of the soul in the tongue, which is why the sage said, "Speak, that I may know thee." Some hold that the art of conversation is to be without art—that it should be neat, not gaudy, like clothing. This holds good for talk between friends. But when held with persons to whom one would show respect, it should be more dignified to answer to the dignity of the person addressed. To be appropriate it should adapt itself to the mind and tone of others. And do not be a critic of words, or you will be taken for a pedant; nor a taxgatherer of ideas, or people will avoid you, or at least sell their thoughts dear. In conversation discretion is more important than eloquence.

· 149 ·

KNOW HOW TO PUT OFF ILLS ON OTHERS. To have a shield against ill will is a great piece of skill in a ruler. It is not the resort of incapacity, as ill-wishers imagine, but is due to the higher policy of having someone to receive the censure of the disaffected and the punishment of universal dislike. Everything cannot turn out well, nor can everyone be satisfied. It is well, therefore, even at the cost of our pride, to have such a scapegoat, a target for unlucky undertakings.

· 150 ·

KNOW HOW TO GET YOUR PRICE FOR THINGS. Their intrinsic value is not sufficient, for not everyone bites at the essence or looks into the interior. Most go with the crowd, and go because they see others go. It is a great stroke of art to show things at true value—at times by praising them (for praise arouses desire), at times by giving them a striking name (which is very useful for putting things at a premium), provided it is done without affectation. Again, it is generally an inducement to profess to supply only to connoisseurs, for all think themselves such, and if not, the sense of want arouses the desire. Never call things easy or common—that makes them depreciated rather than made accessible. All rush after the unusual, which is more appetizing both for the taste and for the intelligence.

· 151 ·

THINK BEFOREHAND. Today for tomorrow, and even for many days hence. The greatest foresight consists in determining beforehand the time of trouble. For the provident there are no mischances and for the careful no narrow escapes. We must not put off thought till we are up to the chin in mire. Mature reflection can get over the most formidable difficulty. "The pillow is a silent Sibyl," and it is better to sleep on things beforehand than lie awake about them afterwards. Many act first and then think later—that is, they think less of consequences than of excuses. Others think neither before nor after. The whole of life should be one course of thought how not to miss the right path. Rumination and foresight enable one to determine the course of life.

· 152 ·

NEVER HAVE A COMPANION WHO OUTSHINES YOU. The more he does so the less desirable a companion he is. The more he excels in quality, the more in reputation; he will always play first fiddle and you second. If you get any consideration, it is only his leavings. The moon shines bright alone among the stars; when the sun rises she becomes either invisible or imperceptible. Never join one that eclipses you but rather one who sets you in a brighter light. By this means the cunning Fabula in Martial's verse was able to appear beautiful and brilliant, owing to the ugliness and disorder of her companions. But one should as little imperil oneself by an evil companion as pay honor to another at the cost of one's own credit. When you are on the way to fortune associate with the eminent, when arrived with the mediocre.

· 153 ·

BEWARE OF ENTERING WHERE THERE IS A GREAT GAP TO BE FILLED. But if you do be sure to surpass your predecessor—merely to equal him requires twice his worth. As it is an artful stroke to arrange it so that one's successor shall cause you to be missed, so it is policy to see that our predecessor does not eclipse us. To fill a great gap is difficult, for the past always seems best, and to equal the predecessor is not enough, since he has the right of first possession. You must therefore possess additional claims to oust the other from his hold on public opinion.

· 154 ·

DO NOT BELIEVE, OR LIKE, LIGHTLY. Maturity of mind is best shown in slow belief. Lying is the usual thing, so then let belief be unusual. He that is lightly led away soon falls into contempt. At the same time, there is no necessity to betray your doubts against the good faith of others. For this adds insult to discourtesy, since you make out your informant to be either deceiver or deceived. Nor is this the only evil. Lack of belief is the mark of the liar, who suffers from two failings: he neither believes nor is believed. Suspension of judgment is prudent in a hearer; the speaker can appeal to his original source of information. There is a similar kind of imprudence in liking too easily, for lies may be told by deeds as well as in words, and this deceit is more dangerous for practical life.

· 155 ·

THE ART OF MASTERING YOUR PASSIONS. If possible, oppose the vulgar advances of passion with prudent reflection. This is not difficult for a truly prudent person. The first step toward mastering a passion is to acknowledge that you are in a passion. By this means you begin the conflict with command over your temper, for one has to regulate one's passion to the exact point that is necessary and no further. This is the art of arts in falling into and getting out of a rage. You should know how and when best to come to a stop—and it is most difficult to halt while running double-time. It is a great proof of wisdom to remain clear-sighted during paroxysms of rage. Every excess of passion is a digression from rational conduct. But by this masterful policy reason will never be transgressed, nor pass the bounds of its own moral wisdom. To keep control of passion one must hold firm the reins of attention; he who can do so will be the first person "wise on horseback," and probably the last.*

· 156 ·

SELECT YOUR FRIENDS. Only after passing the examination of experience and the test of fortune will they be graduates, not only in affection

* Spanish proverb: "No one is wise on horseback."—Ed.

but in discernment. Though this is the most important thing in life, it is the one least cared for. Intelligence brings friends to some, chance to most. Yet a person is judged by his friends, for there was never sympathy between wise men and fools. At the same time, to find pleasure in a person's society is no proof of close friendship: it may come from the pleasantness of his company more than from trust in his capacity. There are some friendships legitimate, others illicit; the latter for pleasure, the former for their fertility of ideas and motives. Few are the friends of a person's innermost self, most those of his circumstances. The insight of a true friend is more useful than the goodwill of others, therefore gain them by choice, not by chance. A wise friend wards off worries, a foolish one brings them about. But do not wish them too much luck, or you may lose them.

· 157 ·

DO NOT MAKE MISTAKES ABOUT CHARACTER. That is the worst and yet easiest error. Better be cheated in the price than in the quality of goods. In dealing with people, more than with other things, it is necessary to look within. To know people is different from knowing things. It is profound philosophy to sound the depths of feeling and distinguish traits of character. People must be studied as deeply as books.

· 158 ·

MAKE USE OF YOUR FRIENDS. This requires all the art of discretion. Some are good far off, some when near. Many are no good at conversation but excellent as correspondents, for distance removes some failings which are unbearable in close proximity to them. Friends are for use even more than for pleasure, for they have the three qualities of the good, or, as some say, of being in general: unity, goodness, and truth. For a friend is all in all. Few are worthy to be good friends, and even these become fewer because people do not know how to pick them out.

Keeping friends is more important than making them. Select those that will wear well—if they are new at first it is some consolation that they will become old. Absolutely the best are those well salted, though they may require soaking in the testing. There is no desert like living without friends. Friendship multiplies the good of life and divides the evil. It is the sole remedy against misfortune, like fresh air to the soul.

· 159 ·

PUT UP WITH FOOLS. The wise are always impatient, for he that increases knowledge increase impatiences with folly. Much knowledge is difficult to satisfy. The first great rule of life, according to Epictetus, is to put up with things—he valued this as half of all wisdom. To put up with all the varieties of folly would need much patience. We often have to put up with most from those on whom we most depend, which is a useful lesson in self-control. Out of patience comes forth peace, the priceless boon that is the happiness of the world. But let him that has no power of patience then retire within himself, though even there he will have to put up with himself.

· 160 ·

BE CAREFUL IN SPEAKING. With your rivals out of prudence, with others for the sake of appearance. There is always time to add a word, never to withdraw one. Talk as if you were making your will: the fewer words the less litigation. In trivial matters exercise yourself for the more weighty matters of speech. Profound secrecy has some of the lustre of the divine. He who speaks quickly soon falls or fails.

· 161 ·

KNOW YOUR PET FAULTS. The most perfect of people has them and is either wedded to them or loves them. They are often faults of intellect, and the greater this is, the greater they are, or at least the more conspicuous. It is not so much that their possessor does not know them, he loves them, which is a double evil because it's an irrational affection for avoidable faults. They are spots on perfection, they displease the onlooker as much as they please the possessor. It is a gallant thing to get clear of them, and so give play to one's other qualities. For all people hit upon such a failing, and on going over your qualifications they will take a long look at this blot and blacken it in as deeply as possible, casting your other talents into the shade.

· 162 ·

HOW TO TRIUMPH OVER YOUR RIVALS AND DETRACTORS. It is not enough to despise them, though this is often wise—a gallant bearing is the essential thing. One cannot praise a person too much who speaks well of them who speak ill of him. There is no more heroic vengeance than that of talents and services that at once conquer and torment the envious. Every success is a further twist of the cord round the neck of those who wish you ill, and an enemy's glory is the rival's hell. The envious die not once, but as often as the envied wins applause. The immortality of his fame is the measure of the other's torture; the one lives in endless honor, the other in endless pain. The clarion of fame announces immortality to the one and death to the other—the slow death of envy long drawn out.

· 163 ·

NEVER—OUT OF SYMPATHY WITH THE UNFORTUNATE—INVOLVE YOURSELF IN THEIR FATE. One person's misfortune is another's luck, for one cannot be lucky without many being unlucky. It is a peculiarity of the unfortunate to arouse people's goodwill, who desire to compensate them for the blows of fortune with their useless favor, and it happens that one who was abhorred by all in prosperity is adored by all in adversity. Vengeance on the wing is exchanged for compassion afoot. Yet it should be noticed how fate shuffles the cards. There are people who always consort with the unlucky, and he that yesterday flew high and happy stands today miserable at their side. That reveals nobility of soul but not worldly wisdom.

· 164 ·

THROW STRAWS IN THE AIR TO TEST THE WIND. Find how things will be received, especially from those whose reception or success is doubtful. One can thus be assured of its turning out well, and an opportunity is provided for going on in earnest or withdrawing entirely. By trying people's intentions in this way, the wise person knows on what ground he stands. This is the great rule of foresight in asking, in desiring, and in ruling.

· 165 ·

WAGE WAR HONORABLY. You may be obliged to wage war but not to use poisoned arrows. Everyone must act as he is, not as others would make him to be. Gallantry in the battle of life wins everyone's praise; one should fight so as to conquer, not alone by force but by the way it is used. A mean victory brings no glory, but rather disgrace. Honor always has the upper hand. An honorable person never uses forbidden weapons, such as using a friendship that's ended for the purposes of a hatred just begun; a confidence must never be used for a vengeance. The slightest taint of treason tarnishes one's good name. In people of honor the smallest trace of meanness repels. The noble and the ignoble should be miles apart. Be able to boast that if gallantry, generosity, and fidelity were lost in the world people would be able to rediscover them in your own heart.

· 166 ·

DISTINGUISH PEOPLE OF WORDS FROM PEOPLE OF DEEDS. Discrimination is important, as in the case of friends, persons, and employments, which all have many varieties. Bad words even without bad deeds are bad enough; good words with bad deeds are worse. One cannot dine off words, which are wind, nor off politeness, which is but polite deceit. To catch birds with a mirror is the ideal snare. It is the vain alone who take their wages in windy words. Words should be the pledges of work, and, like pawn tickets, have their market price. Trees that bear leaves but not fruit usually have no core—know them for what they are, of no use except for shade.

· 167 ·

KNOW HOW TO RELY ON YOURSELF. In great crises there is no better companion than a bold heart, and if it becomes weak it must be strengthened from the neighboring parts. Worries die away for the person who asserts himself. One must not surrender to misfortune or else it would become intolerable. Many people do not help themselves in their troubles and double their weight by not knowing how to bear them. He that knows himself knows how to strengthen his weakness, and the wise person conquers everything, even the stars in their courses.

· 168 ·

DO NOT INDULGE IN THE ECCENTRICITIES OF FOLLY. Like vanity, presumptuousness, egotism, untrustworthiness, capriciousness, obstinacy, fancifulness, theatricalism, whimsy, inquisitiveness, contradiction, and all forms of one-sidedness—they are all monstrosities of impertinence. All deformity of mind is more obnoxious than that of the body, because it violates a higher beauty. Yet who can assist such a complete confusion of mind? Where self-control is wanting, there is no room for others' guidance. Instead of paying attention to other people's real derision, people of this kind blind themselves with the false hope of imaginary applause.

· 169 ·

BE MORE CAREFUL NOT TO MISS ONCE THAN TO HIT A HUNDRED TIMES. No one looks at the blazing sun, but all gaze when it is eclipsed. The common talk does not reckon what goes right but what goes wrong. Evil news carries farther than any applause. Many people are not known to the world till they have left it. All the exploits of a person taken together are not enough to wipe out a single small blemish. Avoid therefore falling into error, knowing that ill will notices every error and no success.

· 170 ·

IN ALL THINGS KEEP SOMETHING IN RESERVE. This is a sure way of keeping up your importance. A person should employ all his capacity and power at once and on every occasion. Even in knowledge there should be a rearguard so that your resources are doubled. One must always have something to resort to when there is fear of a defeat. The reserve is of more importance than the attacking force, for it is distinguished by valor and reputation. Prudence always sets to work with assurance of safety. In this matter the piquant paradox holds true: the half is more than the whole.

· 171 ·

DO NOT WASTE INFLUENCE. The great as friends are for great occasions. One should not make use of great confidence for little things, for that wastes a favor. The emergency anchor should be reserved for the last resort. If you use up the great for little ends what remains afterward? Nothing is more valuable than a protector and nothing costs more nowadays than a favor. It can make or unmake a whole world. It can even support your wits or take them away. As nature and fame are favorable to the wise, so luck is generally envious of them. It is therefore more important to keep the favor of the mighty than goods and chattels.

· 172 ·

NEVER CONTEND WITH SOMEONE WHO HAS NOTHING TO LOSE. By doing so you enter into an unequal conflict. The other enters without anxiety—having lost everything, including shame, he has no further loss to fear. He therefore resorts to all kinds of insolence. One should never expose a valuable reputation to so terrible a risk, least of all what has cost years to gain and may be lost in a moment—a single slight may wipe out much sweat. A person of honor and responsibility has a reputation, because he has much to lose. He balances his own and the other's reputation. He only enters into the contest with the greatest caution, and then goes to work with such circumspection that he gives prudence the opportunity to retire in time and bring his reputation under cover. For even by victory he cannot gain what he has lost by exposing himself to the chances of loss.

· 173 ·

DO NOT BE MADE OF GLASS IN YOUR RELATIONS WITH OTHERS, STILL LESS IN FRIENDSHIP. Some break very easily, and thereby show their want of consistency. They attribute to themselves imaginary offenses and to others oppressive intentions. Their feelings are even more sensitive than the eye itself and must not be touched in jest or in earnest. Motes offend them; they need not wait for beams. Those who consort with them must treat them with the greatest delicacy, have regard to their sensitiveness, and watch their demeanor, since the slightest slight arouses their annoyance. They are mostly very egoistic, slaves of their moods, for the sake of which they cast everything aside. They are worshippers of little nothings. On the other hand, the disposition of the true lover is almost diamond-like: hard and everlasting.

· 174 ·

DO NOT LIVE IN A HURRY. To know how to separate things is to know how to enjoy them. Many people finish their fortune sooner than their life. They run through pleasures without enjoying them, and would like to go back when they find they have overrun the mark. Postilions of life, they increase the ordinary pace of life by the hurry of their own calling. They devour more in one day than they can digest in a whole lifetime; they live in advance of pleasures, eat up the years beforehand, and by their hurry get through everything too soon. Even in the search for knowledge there should be moderation, lest we learn things better left unknown. We have more days to live through than pleasures. Be slow in enjoyment, quick at work, for people see work ended with pleasure, pleasure ended with regret.

· 175 ·

A SOLID PERSON. One who is finds no satisfaction in those that are not. It is a pitiable eminence that is not well founded. Not all are those that seem to be so. Some are sources of deceit—impregnated by chimeras, they give birth to impositions. Others are like them so much that they take more pleasure in a lie (because it promises much) than in the truth (because it performs little). But in the end these caprices come to a bad end, for they have no solid foundation. Only truth can give true reputation; only reality can be of real profit. One deceit needs many others, and so the whole house is built in the air and must soon come to the ground. Unfounded things never reach old age. They promise too much to be much trusted: that cannot be true that proves too much.

· 176 ·

HAVE KNOWLEDGE, OR KNOW THOSE WHO DO. Without intelligence, either one's own or another's, true life is impossible. But many do not know that they do not know, and many think they know when they know nothing. Failings of the intelligence are incorrigible, since those who do not know, do not know themselves, and cannot therefore seek what they lack. Many would be wise if they did not think themselves wise. Thus it happens that though the oracles of wisdom are precious, they are rarely used. To seek advice does not lessen greatness or argue incapacity. On the contrary, to ask advice proves you well advised. Take counsel with reason if you do not wish to court defeat.

· 177 ·

AVOID BEING TOO FAMILIAR WITH OTHERS. Nor should you permit others to be too familiar with you. He that is too familiar loses any superiority his influence gives him and so loses respect. The stars keep their brilliance by not making themselves common. The divine demands decorum. Every familiarity breeds contempt. In human affairs, the more a person shows the less he has, for in open communication you communicate the failings that reserve might keep under cover. Familiarity is never desirable: with superiors because it is dangerous, with inferiors because it is unbecoming, least of all with the common herd, who become insolent from sheer folly—they mistake favor shown them for need felt of them. Familiarity verges on vulgarity.

· 178 ·

TRUST YOUR HEART. Especially when it has been proved. Never deny it a hearing. It is a kind of house oracle that often foretells the things most important. Many have perished because they feared their own heart, but of what use is it to fear it without finding a better remedy? Many are endowed by nature with a heart so true that it always warns them of misfortune and wards off its effects. It is unwise to seek evils, unless you seek to conquer them.

· 179 ·

RETICENCE IS THE SEAL OF CAPACITY. A heart without a secret is an open letter. Where there is a solid foundation secrets can be kept profound—there are specious cellars where important things may be hid. Reticence springs from self-control and to control oneself in this is a true triumph. You must pay ransom to each you tell. The security of wisdom consists in inner temperance. The risk that reticence runs lies in the cross-questioning of others, in the use of contradiction to worm out secrets, in the darts of irony. To avoid these the prudent become more reticent than ever. What must be done need not be said, and what must be said need not be done.

· 180 ·

NEVER GUIDE THE ENEMY TO WHAT HE HAS TO DO. The fool never does what the wise judge wise, because he does not follow up with suitable means. He that is discreet follows still less a plan laid out, or even carried out, by another. One has to discuss matters from both points of view—turn it over on both sides. Judgments vary. Let him that has not decided attend rather to what is possible than what is probable.

· 181 ·

THE TRUTH, BUT NOT THE WHOLE TRUTH. Nothing demands more caution than the truth—it is the lancet of the heart. It requires as much to tell the truth as to conceal it. A single lie destroys a whole reputation for integrity. The deceit is regarded as treason and the deceiver as a traitor, which is worse. Yet not all truths can be spoken, some for our own sake, others for the sake of others.

· 182 ·

A GRAIN OF BOLDNESS IN EVERYTHING. This is an important piece of prudence. You must moderate your opinion of others so that you may not think so high of them as to fear them. The imagination should never yield to the heart. Many appear great till you know them personally, and then dealing with them does more to raise disillusion than esteem. No one oversteps the narrow bounds of humanity—all have their weaknesses either in heart or head. Dignity gives apparent authority, which is rarely accompanied by personal power, for fortune often redresses the height of office by the inferiority of the holder. The imagination always jumps too soon and paints things in brighter colors than the real. It thinks things not as they are but as it wishes them to be. Attentiveness—though disillusioned in the past—soon corrects all that. Yet if wisdom should not be timorous, neither should folly be rash. And if self-reliance helps the ignorant, how much more the brave and wise?

· 183 ·

DO NOT HOLD YOUR VIEWS TOO FIRMLY. Every fool is fully convinced, and everyone fully persuaded is a fool; the more erroneous his judgment the more firmly he holds it. Even in cases of obvious certainty, it is fine to yield. Our reasons for holding the view cannot escape notice, our courtesy in yielding will be recognized. Our obstinacy loses more than our victory gains—that is not to champion truth but rather rudeness. There are some heads of iron most difficult to turn, and add caprice to obstinacy and the sum is a wearisome fool. Steadfastness should be for the will, not for the mind. Yet there are exceptions where one would fail twice, owning oneself wrong both in judgment and in the execution of it.

· 184 ·

DO NOT STAND ON CEREMONY. Even in kings this affectation is renowned for eccentricity. To be punctilious is to be a bore, yet whole nations have this peculiarity. The garb of folly is woven out of such things. Such folk are worshippers of their own dignity, yet show how little it is justified since they fear that the least thing can destroy it. It is right to demand respect, but not to be considered a master of ceremonies. Yet it is true that in order to do without ceremonies one must possess supreme qualities. Neither affect nor despise etiquette—he cannot be great who is great at such little things.

· 185 ·

NEVER STAKE YOUR CREDIT ON A SINGLE CAST OF THE DICE. If it miscarries the damage is irreparable. It may easily happen that you might fail once, especially at first. Circumstances are not always favorable, hence they say, "Every dog has his day." Always connect your second attempt with your first, because whether it succeeds or fails the first will redeem the second. Always have resort to better means and appeal to more resources. Things depend on all sorts of chances. That is why the satisfaction of success is so rare.

· 186 ·

RECOGNIZE FAULTS, HOWEVER HIGHLY PLACED. Integrity can discover vice when clothed in brocade or even crowned with gold, but will not be able to hide its own character for all that. Slavery does not lose its vileness because it is disguised by the nobility of its lord and master. Vices may stand in a high place, but are low for all that. People may see that many a great person has great faults, yet they do not see that he is not great because of them. The example of the great is so specious that it even glosses over viciousness, until it may so affect those who flatter it that they do not notice that what they gloss over in the great they abominate in the lower classes.

· 187 ·

DO PLEASANT THINGS YOURSELF, UNPLEASANT THINGS THROUGH OTHERS. By the one course you gain goodwill, by the other you avoid hatred. A great person takes more pleasure in doing a favor than in receiving one—it is the privilege of his generous nature. One cannot easily cause pain to another without suffering pain either from sympathy or from remorse. In a high position one can only work by means of rewards and punishment, so grant the first yourself, inflict the other through others. Have someone against whom the weapons of discontent, hatred, and slander may be directed. For the rage of the mob is like that of a dog: missing the cause of its pain it turns to bite the whip itself and, though this is not the real culprit, it has to pay the penalty.

· 188 ·

BE THE BEARER OF PRAISE. This increases our credit for good taste, since it shows that we have learned elsewhere to know what is excellent and hence how to prize it in the present company. It gives material for conversation and for imitation and encourages praiseworthy exertions. Besides, this does homage in a very delicate way to the excellences before us. Others do the opposite, they accompany their talk with a sneer, and fancy they flatter those present by belittling the absent. This may serve them with superficial people, who do not notice how cunning it is to speak ill of everyone to everyone else. Many pursue the plan of valuing more highly the mediocrities of the day than the most distinguished exploits of the past. Let the cautious penetrate through these subtleties, and let him not be dismayed by the exaggerations of the one or made overconfident by the flatteries of the other; knowing that both act in the same way by different methods, adapting their talk to the company they are in.

· 189 ·

UTILIZE ANOTHER'S WANTS. The greater his wants the greater the turn of the screw. Philosophers say privation is nonexistent, but statesmen say it is all-embracing, and they are right. Many make ladders to attain their ends out of the wants of others. They make use of the opportunity and tantalize the appetite by pointing out the difficulty of satisfaction. The energy of desire promises more than the inertia of possession. The passion of desire increases with every increase of opposition. It is a subtle point to satisfy the desire and yet preserve the dependence.

· 190 ·

FIND CONSOLATION IN ALL THINGS. Even the useless may find it in being immortal. No trouble without compensation. Fools are held to be lucky, and the good luck of the ugly is proverbial. Be worth little and you will live long—it is the cracked glass that never gets broken, but worries one with its durability. It seems that fortune envies the great, so it equalizes things by giving long life to the useless, a short one to the important. Those who bear the burden come soon to grief, while those who are of no importance live on and on: in one case it appears so, in the other it is so. The unlucky thinks he has been forgotten by both death and fortune.

· 191 ·

DO NOT TAKE PAYMENT IN POLITENESS. This is a kind of fraud. Some do not need exotic herbs for their magic potion, for they can enchant fools by the grace of their salute. Theirs is the Bank of Elegance, and they pay with the wind of fine words. To promise everything is to promise nothing—promises are the pitfalls of fools. The true courtesy is performance of duty; the spurious, and especially the useless, is deceit. It is not respect but rather a means to power. Obeisance is paid not to the man but to his means, and compliments are offered not to the qualities that are recognized but to the advantages that are desired.

· 192 ·

A PEACEFUL LIFE IS A LONG LIFE. To live, let live. Peacemakers not only live, they rule life. Hear, see, and be silent. A day without dispute brings sleep without dreams. Long life and a pleasant one is life enough for two—that is the fruit of peace. He has all that makes nothing of what is nothing to him. There is no greater perversity than to take everything to heart. There is equal folly in troubling our heart about what does not concern us and in not taking to heart what does.

· 193 ·

WATCH OUT FOR PEOPLE WHO BEGIN WITH ANOTHER'S CONCERN TO END WITH THEIR OWN. Watchfulness is the only guard against cunning. Be intent on their intentions. Many succeed in making others do their own affairs, and unless you possess the key to their motives you may at any moment be forced to take their chestnuts out of the fire to the damage of your own fingers.

· 194 ·

HAVE REASONABLE VIEWS OF YOURSELF AND OF YOUR AFFAIRS. This is especially true in the beginning of life. Everyone has a high opinion of himself, especially those who have least ground for it. Everyone dreams of his good luck and thinks himself a marvel. Hope gives rise to extravagant promises that experience does not fulfil. Such idle imaginations merely serve as a wellspring of annoyance when disillusion comes with the true reality. The wise man anticipates such errors. He may always hope for the best, but he always expects the worst, so as to receive what comes with equanimity. True, it is wise to aim high so as to hit your mark, but not so high that you miss your mission at the very beginning of life. This correction of expectations is necessary because before experience comes, expectation is sure to soar too high. The best panacea against folly is prudence. If you know the true sphere of your activity and position, you can reconcile ideals with reality.

· 195 ·

KNOW HOW TO APPRECIATE. There is no one who cannot teach somebody something, and there is no one so excellent that he cannot be excelled. To know how to make use of everyone is useful knowledge. Wise men appreciate everyone, for they see the good in each and know how hard it is to make anything good. Fools depreciate everyone, not recognizing the good and selecting the bad.

· 196 ·

KNOW YOUR RULING STAR. No one is so helpless as not to have a ruling star; if he is unlucky, that is because he does not know it. Some stand high in the favor of princes and potentates without knowing why or wherefore, except that good luck itself has granted them favor on easy terms, merely requiring them to aid it with a little exertion. Others find favor with the wise. One person is better received by one nation than by another, or is more welcome in one city than in another. He finds more luck in one office or position than another, and all this though his qualifications are equal or even identical. Luck shuffles the cards how and when she will. Let each person know his luck as well as his talents, for on this depends whether he loses or wins. Follow your guiding star and help it without mistaking it for any other, for that would be to miss the north, though its neighbor (the polestar) calls us to it with a voice of thunder.

· 197 ·

DO NOT CARRY FOOLS ON YOUR BACK. He that does not know a fool when he sees one is one himself, still more he that knows him but will not keep clear of him. They are dangerous company and ruinous confidants. Even though their own caution and others' care keeps them in bounds for a time, still at length they are sure to do or to say some foolishness that is all the greater for being kept so long in stock. They cannot help another's credit who have none of their own. They are most unlucky, which is the nemesis of fools, and they have to pay for one thing or the other. There is only one thing that is not so bad about them, and this is that though they can be of no use to the wise, they are good as warning signs or as signposts.

· 198 ·

KNOW HOW TO TRANSPLANT YOURSELF. There are nations with whom one must cross their borders to make one's value felt, especially when in great posts. Their native land is always a stepmother to great talents; envy flourishes there on its native soil, and they remember one's small beginnings rather than the greatness one has reached. A needle is appreciated that comes from one end of the world to the other, and a piece of painted glass might outvie the diamond in value if it comes from afar. Everything foreign is respected, partly because it comes from afar, partly because it is ready-made and perfect. We have seen a person once the laughingstock of their village and now the wonder of the whole world, honored by their fellow countrymen and by foreigners—by the latter because they come from afar, by the former because they are seen from afar. The wood statue on the altar is never reverenced by him who knew it as a tree trunk in the garden.

· 199 ·

FIND YOUR PROPER PLACE BY MERIT, NOT BY PRESUMPTION. The true road to respect is through merit, and if industry accompanies merit the path becomes shorter. Integrity alone is not sufficient, push and insistence is degrading, for things that arrive by that means are so sullied that the discredit destroys reputation. The true way is the middle one, halfway between deserving a place and pushing oneself into it.

· 200 ·

LEAVE SOMETHING TO WISH FOR. That way you will not be miserable from too much happiness. The body must respire and the soul aspire. If one possessed all, all would be disillusion and discontent. Even in knowledge there should be always something left to know in order to arouse curiosity and excite hope. Surfeits of happiness are fatal. In giving assistance it is a piece of policy not to satisfy entirely. If there is nothing left to desire, there is everything to fear—an unhappy state of happiness. When desire dies, fear is born.

· 201 ·

THEY ARE ALL FOOLS WHO SEEM SO, AS WELL AS HALF THE REST. Folly arose with the world, and if there be any wisdom it is folly compared with the divine. But the greatest fool is he who thinks he is not one and all others are. To be wise it is not enough to seem wise, least of all to seem so to oneself. He knows who does not think that he knows, and he does not see who does not see that others see. Though all the world is full of fools, there is no one who thinks himself one, or even suspects the fact.

· 202 ·

WORDS AND DEEDS MAKE THE PERFECT PERSON. One should speak well and act honorably; the one is an excellence of the head, the other of the heart, and both arise from nobility of soul. Words are the shadows of deeds—the former are feminine, the latter masculine. It is more important to be renowned than to convey renown. Speech is easy, action hard. Actions are the stuff of life, words its frippery. Eminent deeds endure, striking words pass away. Actions are the fruit of thought; if this is wise, they are effective.

· 203 ·

KNOW THE GREAT PEOPLE OF YOUR AGE. They are not many. There is one phoenix in the whole world, one great general, one perfect orator, one true philosopher in a century, one really illustrious king in several. Mediocrities are as numerous as they are worthless; eminent greatness is rare in every respect, since it needs complete perfection, and the higher the species the more difficult is the highest rank in it. Many have claimed the title *Great,* like Caesar and Alexander, but in vain, for without great deeds the title is a mere breath of air. There have been few Senecas, and fame records but one Apelles.

· 204 ·

ATTEMPT EASY TASKS AS IF THEY WERE DIFFICULT AND DIFFICULT AS IF THEY WERE EASY. In the one case so that confidence may not fall asleep, in the other so that it may not be dismayed. For a thing to remain undone nothing more is needed than to think it done. On the other hand, patient industry overcomes impossibilities. Great undertakings are not to be brooded over, lest their difficulty when seen causes despair.

· 205 ·

KNOW HOW TO PLAY THE CARD OF CONTEMPT. It is a shrewd way of getting things you want, by pretending to depreciate them; generally they are not to be had when sought for, but fall into one's hands when one is not looking for them. As all mundane things are but shadows of the things eternal, they share with shadows this quality, that they flee from him who follows them and follow him that flees from them. Contempt is also the most subtle form of revenge. It is a fixed rule with the wise never to defend themselves with the pen. For such defense always leaves a stain, and does more to glorify one's opponent than to punish his offense. It is a trick of the worthless to stand forth as opponents of great men, so as to win notoriety by a roundabout way, which they would never do by the straight road of merit. There are many we would not have heard of if their eminent opponents had not taken notice of them. There is no revenge like oblivion, through which they are buried in the dust of their unworthiness. An audacious person hopes to make themself eternally famous by setting fire to one of the wonders of the world and of the ages. The art of reproving scandal is to take no notice of it. To combat it damages our own case—even if credited it causes discredit and is a source of satisfaction to our opponent. This shadow of a stain dulls the lustre of our fame, even if it cannot altogether deaden it.

· 206 ·

KNOW THAT THERE ARE VULGAR PEOPLE EVERYWHERE. This is true even in Corinth* itself, even in the highest families. Everyone may try the experiment within his own gates. But there is also such a thing as vulgar opposition to vulgarity, which is worse. This special kind shares all the qualities of the common kind, just as bits of a broken glass, but this kind is still more pernicious; it speaks folly, blames impertinently,

* An ancient Greek city renowned as a place of learning and culture.—Ed.

is a disciple of ignorance, a patron of folly, and past master of scandal. You need not notice what it says, still less what it thinks. It is important to know vulgarity in order to avoid it, whether it is subjective or objective. For all folly is vulgarity, and the vulgar consist of fools.

· 207 ·

BE MODERATE. One has to consider the chance of a mischance. The impulses of the passions cause prudence to slip, and there is the risk of ruin. A moment of wrath or of pleasure carries you on farther than many hours of calm, and often a short diversion may put a whole life to shame. The cunning of others uses such moments of temptation to search the recesses of the mind. They use such thumbscrews to test your best sense of caution. Moderation serves as a counterplot, especially in sudden emergencies. Much thought is needed to prevent a passion taking the bit in the teeth, and he is doubly wise who is wise on horseback. He who knows the danger may with care pursue his journey. As light as a word may appear to him who throws it out, it may import much to him that hears it and ponders on it.

· 208 ·

DO NOT DIE OF THE FOOLS' DISEASE. The wise generally die after they have lost their reason, fools before they have found it. To die of the fools' disease is to die of too much thought. Some die because they think and feel too much, others live because they do not think and feel at all. The first are fools because they die of sorrow, the others because they do not. A fool is he that dies of too much knowledge. Thus some die because they are too knowing, others because they are not knowing enough. Yet though many die like fools, few die fools.

· 209 ·

KEEP YOURSELF FREE FROM COMMON FOLLIES. This is a special stroke of policy. They are of special power because they are common, so that many who would not be led away by any individual folly cannot escape the universal failing. Among these are to be counted the common prejudice of anyone who is satisfied with his fortune, however great, or unsatisfied with his intellect, however poor it is. Or again, that each, being discontented with his own lot, envies that of others. Or further, that persons of today praise the things of yesterday, and those here the things there. Everything past seems best and everything distant is more valued. He is as great a fool that laughs at everything as is he that weeps at everything.

· 210 ·

KNOW HOW TO PLAY THE CARD OF TRUTH. It is dangerous, yet a good person cannot avoid speaking it. But great skill is needed here. The most expert doctors of the soul pay great attention to the means of sweetening the pill of truth. For when it deals with the destroying of illusion it is the quintessence of bitterness. A pleasant manner has here an opportunity for a display of skill—with the same truth it can flatter one and fell another to the ground. Matters of today should be treated as if they were long past. For those who can understand, a word is sufficient, and if it does not suffice, it is a case for silence. Princes must not be cured with bitter draughts, so it is desirable in their case to gild the pill of disillusion.

· 211 ·

IN HEAVEN ALL IS BLISS. And in hell all misery. On earth, between the two, both one thing and the other. We stand between the two extremes, and therefore share both. Fate varies—all is not good luck nor all mischance. This world is merely zero—by itself it is of no value—but with heaven in front of it, it means much. Indifference at its ups and downs is prudent, nor is there any novelty for the wise. Our life gets as complicated as a comedy as it goes on, but the complications get gradually resolved—see that the curtain comes down on a good denouement.

·212·

KEEP TO YOURSELF THE FINAL TOUCHES OF YOUR ART. This is a maxim of the great masters who pride themselves on this subtlety in teaching their pupils: one must always remain superior, remain master. One must teach an art artfully. The source of knowledge need not be pointed out no more than that of giving. By this means a person preserves the respect and the dependence of others. In amusing and teaching, you must observe the rule: keep up expectation and advance in perfection. To keep a reserve is a great rule for life and for success, especially for those in high places.

·213·

KNOW HOW TO CONTRADICT. A chief means of finding things out—to embarrass others without being embarrassed. The true thumbscrew, it brings the passions into play. A little disbelief makes people spit up secrets. It is the key to a locked up heart, and with great subtlety makes a double trial of both mind and will. A sly depreciation of another's mysterious word scents out the profoundest secrets; some sweet bait brings them into the mouth till they fall from the tongue and are caught in the net of astute deceit. By reserving your attention the other becomes less attentive, and lets his thoughts appear while otherwise his heart were inscrutable. An affected doubt is the subtlest picklock that curiosity can use to find out what it wants to know. Also in learning it is a subtle plan of the pupil to contradict the master, who thereupon takes pains to explain the truth more thoroughly and with more force, so that a moderate contradiction produces complete instruction.

· 214 ·

Do not turn one blunder into two. It is quite usual to commit four blunders in order to remedy one, or to excuse one piece of impertinence by still another. Folly is either related to or identical with the family of lies, for in both cases it needs many to support one. The worst of a bad case is having to fight it, and worse than the ill itself is not being able to conceal it. The annuity of one failing serves to support many others. A wise person may make one slip but never two, and that only in running not while standing still.

· 215 ·

Watch out for those who act on second thoughts. It is a device of business people to put the opponent off his guard before attacking him, and thus to conquer by being defeated. They dissemble their desire so as to attain it. They put themselves second so as to come out first. This method rarely fails if it is not noticed. Let therefore the attention never sleep when the intention is so wide awake. And if the other puts himself second so to hide his plan, put yourself first to discover it. Prudence can discern the artifices that such a man uses, and notices the pretexts he puts forward to gain his ends. He aims at one thing to get another, then he turns round smartly and fires straight at his target. It is good to know what you grant him, and at times it is desirable to let him understand that you understand.

· 216 ·

Be expressive. This depends not only on the clearness but also on the vivacity of your thoughts. Some have an easy conception but a hard labor, for without clarity the children of the mind—thoughts and judgments—cannot be brought into the world. Many have a capacity like that of vessels with a large mouth and a small vent. Others say more than they think. Resolution for the will, expression for the thought—both are great gifts. Plausible minds are applauded, yet confused ones are often venerated just because they are not understood—at times obscurity is convenient if you wish to avoid vulgarity. How will the audience understand someone who does not connect any definite idea with what he is talking about?

·217·

NEITHER LOVE NOR HATE FOREVER. Trust the friends of today as if they will be enemies tomorrow, and that of the worst kind. As this happens in reality, let it happen in your precaution. Do not put weapons in the hand for deserters from friendship to wage war with. On the other hand, leave the door of reconciliation open for enemies, and if it is also the gate of generosity so much the more safe. The vengeance of long ago is at times the torment of today, and the joy over the ill we have done is turned to grief.

·218·

NEVER ACT FROM OBSTINACY BUT FROM KNOWLEDGE. All obstinacy is an evil tumor on the mind, a grandchild of passion that never did anything right. There are people who make a war out of everything, real bandits of social intercourse. All that they undertake must end in victory. They do not know how to get on in peace. Such people are fatal when they rule and govern, for they make government a rebellion and enemies out of those they should regard as children. They try to effect everything with strategy and treat it as the fruit of their skill. But when others have recognized their perverse humor, they revolt against them and learn to overturn their chimerical plans. They succeed in nothing but only heap up a mass of troubles, since everything serves to increase their disappointment. They have a head turned and a heart spoilt. Nothing can be done with such monsters except to flee from them—

even the savagery of barbarians is easier to bear than their loathsome nature.

· 219 ·

DO NOT PASS FOR A HYPOCRITE. Though nowadays, such people are indispensable. Be considered prudent rather than astute. Sincerity in behavior pleases all, though not all can show it in their own affairs. Sincerity should not degenerate into simplicity nor sagacity into cunning. Be respected as wise rather than feared as sly. The openhearted are loved but often deceived. The great art consists in disclosing what is thought to be deceit. Simplicity flourished in the golden age, cunning in these days of iron. The reputation of someone who knows what he has to do is honorable and inspires confidence, but to be considered a hypocrite is deceptive and arouses mistrust.

· 220 ·

IF YOU CANNOT CLOTHE YOURSELF IN LION SKIN USE FOX PELT. To follow the times is to lead them. He that gets what he wants never loses his reputation. Use cleverness when force will not do. Take one way or another, the king's highway of valor or the bypath of cunning. Skill has effected more than force, and astuteness has conquered courage more often than the other way around. When you cannot get something, that is the time to despise it.

· 221 ·

DO NOT SEIZE OCCASIONS TO EMBARRASS YOURSELF OR OTHERS. There are some people who are stumbling blocks of good manners either for themselves or for others. They are always on the verge of some stupidity. You meet with them easily and part from them uneasily.

A hundred annoyances a day is nothing to them. Their humor always strokes the wrong way since they contradict all and everything. They put on the judgment cap backwards and thus condemn all. Yet the greatest test of others' patience and prudence are just those who do no good and speak ill of all. There are many monsters in the wide realm of indecorum.

· 222 ·

RESERVE IS PROOF OF PRUDENCE. The tongue is a wild beast—once let loose it is difficult to chain. It is the pulse of the soul by which wise men judge its health. By this pulse a careful observer feels every movement of the heart. The worst is that he who should be most reserved is the least. The sage saves himself from worries and embarrassments, and shows his mastery over himself. He goes his way carefully, a Janus of impartiality, an Argus of watchfulness. Certainly Momus would have better placed the eyes in the hand than the window in the breast.*

· 223 ·

DO NOT BE ECCENTRIC, NEITHER FROM AFFECTATION NOR CARELESS-NESS. Many have some remarkable and individual quality leading to eccentric actions. These are more defects than excellent differences. And just as some are known for some special ugliness, so these for something repellant in their outward behavior. Such eccentricities simply serve as trademarks through their atrocious singularity—they cause either derision or ill will.

---

* Janus is the ancient Roman god of doorways, who is usually often depicted as one-headed but with two faces, looking in opposite directions. Argus is a mythological giant with a hundred eyes. In a story by the classical Greek writer Lucian, the Greek god Momus ridiculed the god Hephaistos for making a man without a window in his breast.—Ed.

· 224 ·

NEVER TAKE THINGS AGAINST THE GRAIN, NO MATTER HOW THEY COME. Everything has a smooth and a seamy side. The best of weapons wounds if taken by the blade, while the enemy's spear may be our best protection if taken by the staff. Many things cause pain that would cause pleasure if you regarded their advantages. There is a favorable and an unfavorable side to everything—cleverness consists in finding out the favorable. The same thing looks quite different in another light; look at it therefore on its best side and do not exchange good for evil. Thus it happens that many find joy, many grief, in everything. This remark is a great protection against the frowns of fortune, and a weighty rule of life for all times and all conditions.

· 225 ·

KNOW YOUR CHIEF FAULT. There is no one lives who has not in himself a counterbalance to his most conspicuous merit, and if it is nourished by desire it may grow to be a tyrant. Commence war against it, summoning prudence as your ally. The first thing to do is to make it public, for an evil once known is soon conquered, especially when the one afflicted regards it in the same light as the onlookers. To be master of oneself one should know oneself. If the chief imperfection is surrendered, the rest will also come to an end.

· 226 ·

TAKE CARE TO BE OBLIGING. Most talk and act, not as they are, but as they are obliged. To persuade people of the bad is easy for anyone, since the bad is easily credited even when it is incredible. The best we have depends on the opinion of others. Some are satisfied if they have right on their side, but that is not enough, for it must be assisted by energy. To oblige people often costs little and helps much. With words you may purchase deeds. In this great house of the world there is no chamber so hidden that it may not be wanted one day in the year, and then you would miss it however little its worth. Everyone speaks of a subject according to his feelings.

· 227 ·

DO NOT BE THE SLAVE OF FIRST IMPRESSIONS. Some marry the very first account they hear, all others must live with them as concubines. But as a lie has swift legs, the truth with them can find no lodging. We should neither satisfy our will with the first object nor our mind with the first proposition—for that is superficial. Many are like new casks who keep the scent of the first liquor they hold, be it good or bad. If this superficiality becomes known, it becomes fatal, for it then gives opportunity for cunning mischief. The evil-minded hasten to color the mind of the gullible. Always therefore leave room for a second hearing. Alexander always kept one ear for the other side. Wait for the second or even third edition of news. To be the slave of your first impressions shows lack of capacity, and is not far from being the slave of your passions.

· 228 ·

DO NOT BE A SCANDALMONGER. Still less pass for one, for that means to be considered a slanderer. Do not be witty at the cost of others; it is easy but hateful. Everyone will have their revenge on such a person by speaking ill of him and, as they are many and he but one, he is more likely to be overcome than they convinced. Evil should never be our pleasure and therefore never our theme. The backbiter is always hated, and if now and then one of the great consorts with him it is less from pleasure in his sneers than from esteem for his insight. He that speaks ill will always hear worse.

· 229 ·

PLAN OUT YOUR LIFE WISELY. Not as chance will have it, but with prudence and foresight. Without amusements it is wearisome, like a long journey where there are no inns—manifold knowledge gives manifold pleasure. The first day's journey of a noble life should be passed in conversing with the dead: we live to know and to know ourselves, hence true books make us truly human. The second day should be spent with the living, seeing and noticing all the good in the world. Everything is not to be found in a single country. The Universal Father has divided his gifts and at times has given the richest dowry to the ugliest. The third day is entirely for oneself. The greatest happiness is to be a philosopher.

· 230 ·

OPEN YOUR EYES EARLY. Not all who see have their eyes open, nor do all those see who look. To come up to things too late is more worry than help. Some just begin to see when there is nothing more to see: they pull their houses down about their heads before they come to themselves. It is difficult to give understanding to those who have no power of will, still more difficult to give power of will to those who have no understanding. Those who surround them play a game of blindman's buff with them, making them the butts of jokes. Because they are hard of hearing, they do not open their eyes to see. There are often those who encourage such insensibility because their very existence depends on it. It is an unhappy steed whose rider is blind: it will never grow sleek.

· 231 ·

NEVER LET THINGS BE SEEN HALF-FINISHED. They can only be enjoyed when complete. All beginnings are misshapen, and this deformity sticks in the imagination. The recollection of having seen a thing imperfect disturbs our enjoyment of it when completed. To swallow something great at one gulp may disturb the judgment of the separate parts, but satisfies the taste. Before a thing is manifest, it is nothing, and while it is in process of being it is still nothing. To see the tastiest dishes prepared arouses disgust rather than appetite. Let each great master take care not to let his work be seen in its embryonic stages—they might take this lesson from Mother Nature, who never brings the child to the light till it is fit to be seen.

· 232 ·

HAVE A TOUCH OF BUSINESS SENSE. Life should not be all thought, there should be action as well. Very wise folk are generally easily deceived, for while they know out-of-the-way things they do not know the ordinary things of life, which are of real necessity. The observation of higher things leaves them no time for things close at hand. Since they do not know the very first thing they should know—and what everybody knows so well—they are either esteemed or thought ignorant by the superficial multitude. Let therefore the prudent take care to have something of the businessman about him—enough to prevent him being deceived and so laughed at. Be a person adapted to the daily round, which if not the highest is the most necessary thing in life. Of what use is knowledge if it is not practical, and to know how to live is nowadays the true knowledge.

· 233 ·

DO NOT LET THE MORSELS YOU OFFER BE DISTASTEFUL. Otherwise they give more discomfort than pleasure. Some annoy when attempting to please, because they take no account of varieties of taste. What is flattery to one is an offence to another, and in attempting to be useful you may become insulting. It often costs more to displease someone than it would have cost to please him—you thereby lose both gift and thanks because you have lost the compass that steers for pleasure. If you do not know another's taste, you do not know how to please him. Thus it happens that many insult where they mean to praise, and get soundly punished, and rightly so. Others desire to charm by their conversation, and only succeed in boring by their babble.

· 234 ·

NEVER TRUST YOUR HONOR TO ANOTHER, UNLESS YOU HAVE HIS IN PLEDGE. Arrange that silence is a mutual advantage, disclosure a danger to both. Where honor is at stake you must act with a partner, so that each must be careful of the other's honor for the sake of his own. Never fully entrust your honor to another, but if you have to, let caution surpass prudence. Let the danger be in common and the risk mutual, so that your partner cannot turn king's evidence.

· 235 ·

KNOW HOW TO ASK. With some nothing is easier, with others nothing is so difficult. For there are men who cannot refuse—with them no skill is required. But with others their first word at all times is *no*—with them great art is required, and with everyone pick the right moment. Surprise them when they are in a pleasant mood, when a repast of body or soul has just left them refreshed—but only if their shrewdness has not anticipated your cunning. The days of joy are the days of favor, for joy overflows from the inner person into the outward creation. It is no use to apply when another has just been refused, since the reticence to saying *no* has just been overcome. Nor is it a good time after sorrow. To oblige a person beforehand is a sure way, unless he is base and mean.

· 236 ·

MAKE AN OBLIGATION BEFOREHAND OF WHAT WOULD HAVE TO BE A REWARD AFTERWARD. This is a stroke of subtle policy. To grant favors before they are deserved is a proof of being obliging. Favors thus granted beforehand have two great advantages: the promptness of the gift obliges the recipient more strongly, and the same gift that would afterward be merely a reward is beforehand an obligation. This is a subtle means of transforming obligations, since that which would force you to reward someone is changed into one that obliges them to satisfy their obligation. But this is only suitable for people who feel obligation, since with people of lower stamp the honorarium paid beforehand acts rather as a bit than as a spur.

· 237 ·

NEVER SHARE THE SECRETS OF YOUR SUPERIORS. You may think you will share pears, but you will only share parings. Many have been ruined by being confidants: they are like sops of bread used like spoons, they run the same risk of being eaten up afterwards. It is no favor to a prince to share a secret—it is only a relief. Many break the mirror that reminds them of their ugliness. We do not like seeing those who have seen us as we are, nor is he seen in a favorable light who has seen us in an unfavorable one. No one ought to be too much beholden to us, least of all one of the great, unless it is for favors done for him rather than for favors received. Especially dangerous are secrets entrusted to friends. When you communicate a secret to someone you make yourself his slave. With a prince this is an intolerable position that cannot last; he will desire to recover his lost liberty, and to gain it he will overturn everything, including right and reason. Accordingly, neither tell secrets nor listen to them.

· 238 ·

KNOW WHAT IS LACKING IN YOURSELF. Many would have been great people if they had not had something wanting, without which they could not rise to the height of perfection. It is remarkable that some people could be much better if they could be just a little better in something. They do not perhaps take themselves seriously enough to do justice to their great abilities. Some are lacking geniality of disposition, a quality which their entourage soon find want of, especially if they are in high office. Some are without organizing ability, others lack moderation. In all such cases a careful person may make of habit a second nature.

· 239 ·

DO NOT BE OVERLY CRITICAL. It is much more important to be sensible. To know more than is necessary blunts your weapons, for fine points generally bend or break. Commonsense truth is the surest. It is well to know but not to niggle. Lengthy comment leads to disputes. It is much better to have sound sense, which does not wander from the matter in hand.

· 240 ·

MAKE USE OF FOLLY. The wisest person plays this card at times. Sometimes the greatest wisdom lies in seeming not to be wise. You need not be unwise, but merely affect unwisdom. To be wise with fools and foolish with the wise is of little use; speak to each in his own language. He is no fool who affects folly, but he is who suffers from it. Ingenious folly, rather than simple affect, is the true foolishness, since cleverness is at such a high pitch. To be well liked one must dress in the skin of the simplest of animals.

· 241 ·

PUT UP WITH MOCKERY BUT DO NOT PRACTICE IT YOURSELF. The first is a form of courtesy, the second may lead to embarrassment. To snarl at playful jokes seems beastly. Audacious mocking is delightful and to stand for it proves your power. To show oneself annoyed causes others to be annoyed. Best leave it alone—that is the surest way of avoiding fitting the fool's cap. The most serious matters have arisen out of jests. Nothing requires more tact and attention. Before you begin to joke know how far the subject of your joke is able to bear it.

· 242 ·

PUSH ADVANTAGES. Some put all their strength in the commencement and never carry a thing to conclusion. They invent but never execute. These be ambiguous spirits—they obtain no fame for they sustain no game to the end. Everything ends at the first stop. In some this arises from impatience, which is the failing of the Spaniards, as patience is the virtue of the Belgians. The latter bring things to an end, the former come to an end with things. They sweat away until the obstacle is overcome, but then they are content—they do not know how to push the victory home. They prove that they can but will not. This shows that they are either incapable or unreliable. If the undertaking is good, why not finish it? If it is bad, why undertake it? Strike down your quarry, if you are wise—do not be content merely to flush it out.

· 243 ·

DO NOT BE TOO MUCH OF A DOVE. Alternate the cunning of the serpent with the candor of the dove. Nothing is easier than to deceive an honest man. He believes in much who lies about nothing; he who does no deception has much confidence. To be deceived is not always due to stupidity, it may arise from sheer goodness. There are two sets of people who can guard themselves from injury: those who have learned by experiencing it at their own cost and those who have observed it at the cost of others. Prudence should use as much suspicion as subtlety uses snares, and none need be so good as to enable others to do him ill. Combine in yourself the dove and the serpent, not as a monster but as a prodigy.

· 244 ·

CREATE A FEELING OF OBLIGATION. Some transform favors received into favors bestowed, and seem—or let it be thought—that they are doing a favor when receiving one. There are some so astute that they get honor by asking, and buy their own advantage with applause from others. They manage matters so cleverly that they seem to be doing others a service when receiving one from them. They transpose the order of obligation with extraordinary skill, or at least render it doubtful who has obliged whom. They buy the best by praising it, and make a flattering honor out of the pleasure they express. They oblige by their courtesy, and thus make people beholden for what they themselves should be indebted. In this way they conjugate "to oblige" in the active instead of in the passive voice, thereby proving themselves better politicians than grammarians. This is a subtle piece of finesse, but even greater is to perceive it, and to retaliate on such fools' bargains by paying in their own coin, and so come into your own again.

· 245 ·

HAVE ORIGINAL AND OUT-OF-THE-WAY VIEWS. These are signs of superior ability. We do not think much of someone who never contradicts us; that is not a sign he loves us but rather that he loves himself. Do not be deceived by flattery and thereby have to pay for it, rather condemn it. Besides, you may be given credit for being criticized by some, especially if they are those of whom the good speak ill. On the contrary, it should disturb us if our affairs please everyone, for that is a sign that they are of little worth. Perfection is for the few.

· 246 ·

NEVER OFFER SATISFACTION UNLESS IT IS DEMANDED. And if they do demand it, it is a kind of crime to give more than necessary. To excuse oneself before there is occasion is to accuse oneself. To draw blood in full health gives the hint to ill will. An excuse unexpected arouses suspicion from its slumbers. Nor need a shrewd person show himself aware of another's suspicion, which is equivalent to seeking out offense. He had best disarm distrust by the integrity of his conduct.

· 247 ·

KNOW A LITTLE MORE, LIVE A LITTLE LESS. Some say the opposite. To be at ease is better than to be at business. Nothing really belongs to us but time, which you have even if you have nothing else. It is equally unfortunate to waste your precious life in mechanical tasks or in a profusion of too important work. Do not heap up occupation and thereby envy, otherwise you complicate life and exhaust your mind. Some wish to apply the same principle to knowledge, but unless one knows one does not truly live.

· 248 ·

DO NOT GO WITH THE LATEST SPEAKER. There are people who go by the latest thing they have heard, and thereby go to irrational extremes. Their feelings and desires are made of wax; the last comer stamps them with his seal and obliterates all previous impressions. These people never gain anything, for they lose everything so soon. Everyone dyes them with his own color. They are of no use as confidants; they remain children their whole life. Owing to this instability of feeling and voli-tion, they stumble along, crippled in will and thought, tottering from one side of the road to the other.

· 249 ·

NEVER BEGIN LIFE WITH WHAT SHOULD END IT. Many take their amusement at the beginning, putting off anxiety to the end; but the essential should come first and accessories afterwards if there is room. Others wish to triumph before they have fought. Others again begin with learning things of little consequence and leave studies that would bring them fame and gain to the end of life. Another is just about to make his fortune when he disappears from the scene. Method is essen-tial for knowledge and for life.

· 250 ·

WHEN TO TURN THE CONVERSATION AROUND. When they talk malice. With some everything goes in reverse: their *no* is *yes* and their *yes* is *no*. If they speak ill of something it is the highest praise. For what they want for themselves they depreciate to others. To praise a thing is not always to speak well of it. For some avoid praising what's good by praising what's bad. Nothing is good for him for whom nothing is bad.

· 251 ·

USE HUMAN MEANS AS IF THERE WERE NO DIVINE ONES, AND DIVINE MEANS AS IF THERE WERE NO HUMAN ONES. A masterful rule, which needs no comment.

· 252 ·

NEITHER BELONG ENTIRELY TO YOURSELF NOR ENTIRELY TO OTHERS. Both are mean forms of tyranny. To desire to be all for oneself is the same as desiring to have all for oneself. Such people will not yield the least bit or lose the smallest portion of their comfort. They are rarely beholden, lean on their own luck, and their crutch generally breaks. It is convenient at times to belong to others so that others may belong to us. And he that holds public office is no more nor less than a public slave; let a man give up both berth and burden, as the old woman said to Hadrian.* On the other hand, some people are all for others—this is folly, which always flies to extremes, and in this case in a most unfortunate manner. No day, no hour, is their own. They so much belong to others that they may be called the slaves of all. This applies even to knowledge, where a person may know everything for others and nothing for himself. A shrewd person knows that others, when they seek him, do not seek *him* but their advantage in him and by him.

· 253 ·

DO NOT EXPLAIN TOO MUCH. Most people do not esteem what they understand and venerate what they do not see. To be valued things should cost dear; what is not understood becomes overrated. You have to appear wiser and more prudent than is required by the people you are dealing with if you want to give a high opinion of yourself. Yet in this there should be moderation and no excess. And though with sensible people common sense holds its own, with most people a little elaboration is necessary. Give them no time for criticizing—occupy them with discerning your meaning. Many praise a thing without being able to tell why, if asked. The reason is that they venerate the unknown as a mystery, and praise it because they hear it praised.

· 254 ·

NEVER DESPISE AN EVIL, HOWEVER SMALL. They never come alone, they are linked together like pieces of good fortune. Fortune and mis-

---

* This refers to a story about the Roman emperor Hadrian who when confronted by an old woman with a petition dismissed her saying he didn't have time to consider it. She retorted, "Then give up your berth." Hadrian recognized the justice in this and passed judgment on her petition on the spot. —Ed.

fortune generally go to find their fellows. Hence all avoid the unlucky and associate with the fortunate. Even the doves with all their innocence resort to the whitest walls. Everything fails with the unfortunate—himself, his words, and his luck. Do not wake misfortune when she sleeps. One slip is a little thing, yet some fatal loss may follow it till you do not know where it will end. For just as no happiness is perfect, so no piece of bad luck is complete. Use patience with what comes from above, prudence with that from below.

· 255 ·

DO GOOD A LITTLE AT A TIME, BUT OFTEN. One should never give beyond the possibility of return. He who gives much does not give but sells. Nor drain gratitude to the dregs, for when the recipient sees all return is impossible he breaks off correspondence. With many people it is not necessary to do more than overburden them with favors to lose them altogether; they cannot repay you, and so they retire, preferring rather to be enemies than perpetual debtors. The idol never wishes to see before him the sculptor who shaped him, nor does the benefited wish to see his benefactor always before his eyes. There is a great subtlety in giving what costs little yet is much desired, so that it is esteemed the more.

· 256 ·

GO PREPARED. Go armed against discourtesy, faithlessness, presumption, and all other kinds of folly. There is much of it in the world, and prudence lies in avoiding meeting with it. Arm yourself each day before the mirror of attention with the weapons of defense. Thus you will beat down the attacks of folly. Be prepared for the occasion, and do not expose your reputation to vulgar contingencies. Armed with prudence, a person cannot be disarmed by impertinence. The road of human intercourse is difficult, for it is full of ruts that may jolt our reputation. Best to take a byway, taking Ulysses as a model of shrewdness. Feigned misunderstanding is of great value in such matters. Aided by politeness it helps us over all, and is often the only way out of difficulties.

· 257 ·

NEVER LET MATTERS COME TO A BREAKING POINT. For our reputation always comes out injured. Everyone may be of importance as an enemy if not as a friend. Few can do us good, almost any can do us harm. In Jove's bosom itself even his eagle never nestles securely from the day he has quarreled with a beetle. Hidden foes use the paw of the declared enemy to stir up the fire, and meanwhile they lie in ambush for such an occasion. Friends provoked become the bitterest of enemies. They cover their own failings with the faults of others. Everyone speaks as things seem to him, and things seem as he wishes them to appear. Everyone will blame us at the beginning for want of foresight, at the end for lack of patience, at all times for imprudence. If, however, a breach is inevitable, let it be rather excused as a slackening of friendship than by an outburst of wrath. This is a good application of the saying about a good retreat.*

· 258 ·

FIND SOMEONE TO SHARE YOUR TROUBLES WITH. You will never be all alone, even in dangers, nor bear all the burden of hate. Some think by their high position that they can carry off the whole glory of success, and find that they have to bear the whole humiliation of defeat. In this way they have no one to excuse them, no one to share the blame. Neither fate nor the mob are so bold against two. Hence the wise physician, if he has failed to cure, looks out for someone who, under the name of a consultation, may help him carry out the corpse. Share

* See maxim 38.—Ed.

weight and woe, for misfortune falls with double force on him that stands alone.

· 259 ·

ANTICIPATE INJURIES AND TURN THEM INTO FAVORS. It is wiser to avoid than to revenge them. It is an uncommon piece of shrewdness to change a rival into a confidant, or transform into guards of honor those who were aiming to attack us. It helps much to know how to oblige, for he leaves no time for injuries who fills time up with gratitude. That is true *savoir faire,* to turn anxieties into pleasures. Try and make a confidential relation out of ill will itself.

· 260 ·

WE BELONG TO NO ONE AND NO ONE TO US, ENTIRELY. Neither relationship nor friendship nor the most intimate connection is sufficient to effect this. To give one's whole confidence is quite different from giving one's regard. The closest intimacy has its exceptions, without which the laws of friendship would be broken. The friend always keeps one secret to himself, and even the son always hides something from his father. Some things are kept from one that are revealed to another and vice versa. In this way one reveals all and conceals all, by making a distinction among the persons with whom we are connected.

· 261 ·

DO NOT FOLLOW UP A FOLLY. Many make an obligation out of a blunder, and because they have entered the wrong path they think it proves their strength of character to go on in it. Within they regret their error, while outwardly they excuse it. At the beginning of their mistake they were regarded as inattentive, in the end as fools. Neither an unconsidered promise nor a mistaken resolution are really binding. Yet some continue in their folly and prefer to be constant fools.

· 262 ·

BE ABLE TO FORGET. It is more a matter of luck than of skill. The things we remember best are those better forgotten. Memory is not only unruly, leaving us in the lurch when most needed, but stupid as well, putting its nose into places where it is not wanted. In painful things it is active, but neglectful in recalling the pleasurable. Very often the only remedy for the trouble is to forget it, and all we forget is the remedy. Nevertheless one should cultivate good habits of memory, for it is capable of making existence a paradise or an inferno. The happy are an exception who enjoy innocently their simple happiness.

· 263 ·

MANY THINGS OF TASTE ONE SHOULD NOT POSSESS ONESELF. One enjoys them better if they are another's rather than one's own. The owner has the good of them the first day, for all the rest of the time they are for others. You take a double enjoyment in other men's property, being without fear of spoiling it and with the pleasure of novelty. Everything tastes better for having been without it—even water from another's well tastes like nectar. Possession hinders enjoyment and increases annoyance, whether you lend or keep. You gain nothing except keeping things for or from others, and by this means gain more enemies than friends.

· 264 ·

HAVE NO CARELESS DAYS. Fate loves to play tricks, and will heap up chances to catch us unawares. Our intelligence, prudence, and courage, even our beauty, must always be ready for trial. For their day of careless trust will be that of their discredit. Care always fails just when it was most wanted. It is thoughtlessness that trips us up into destruction. Accordingly, it is a piece of military strategy to put perfections to their trial when unprepared. The days of parade are watched and are allowed to pass, but the day is chosen when least expected so as to put valor to the severest test.

· 265 ·

SET DIFFICULT TASKS FOR THOSE UNDER YOU. Many have proved themselves able at once when they had to deal with a difficulty, just as fear of drowning makes a person into a swimmer. In this way, many have discovered their own courage, knowledge, or tact, which but for the opportunity would have been forever buried beneath their lack of initiative. Dangerous situations are the occasions to create a name for oneself, and if a noble mind sees honor at stake, he will do the work of thousands. Queen Isabella the Catholic knew well this rule of life (as well as all the others) and to a shrewd favor of this kind the Great Captain* won his fame, and many others earned an undying name. By this great art she made great men.

· 266 ·

DO NOT BECOME BAD FROM SHEER GOODNESS. That is, by never getting angry. Such people without feeling are scarcely to be considered human. It does not always arise from laziness, but from sheer inability. To feel strongly on occasion shows personality; birds soon mock at the scarecrow. It is a sign of good taste to combine bitter and sweet. All sweets is diet for children and fools. It is a great evil to sink into such insensibility out of too great goodness.

* "El Gran Capitan," a reference to the Spanish general Gonzalo Fernandez de Cordoba (1453–1515), who commanded the Spanish army against Charles VIII of France.—Ed.

· 267 ·

SILKEN WORDS, SUGARED MANNERS. Arrows pierce the body, insults the soul. Sweet pastry perfumes the breath. It is a great art in life to know how to sell wind. Most things are paid for in words, and by them you can remove impossibilities. Thus we deal in air, and a royal breath can produce courage and power. Always have your mouth full of candies to sweeten your words, so that even your enemies enjoy them. To please one must be peaceful.

· 268 ·

THE WISE DO AT ONCE WHAT THE FOOL DOES LATER. Both do the same thing—the only difference lies in the time they do it: the one at the right time, the other at the wrong. Who starts out with his mind topsy-turvy will so continue till the end. He catches by the foot what he ought to knock on the head, he turns right into left, and in all his acts is immature. There is only one way to turn him in the right direction, and that is to force him to do what he might have done of his own accord. The wise man, on the other hand, sees at once what must be done sooner or later, so he does it willingly and gains honor thereby.

· 269 ·

MAKE USE OF THE NOVELTY OF YOUR POSITION. For people are valued while they are new. Novelty pleases all because it is uncommon, taste is refreshed, and a brand new mediocrity is thought more of than accustomed excellence. Ability wears away by use and becomes old. However, know that the glory of novelty is short-lived. After four days respect is gone. Accordingly, learn to utilize the first fruits of appreciation, and seize during the rapid passage of applause all that can be put to use. For once the heat of novelty is over, the passion cools and the appreciation of novelty is exchanged for distaste at the customary. Believe that everything has its season, which soon passes.

· 270 ·

Do NOT CONDEMN ALONE THAT WHICH PLEASES ALL. There must be something good in a thing that pleases so many—even if it cannot be explained it is certainly enjoyed. Peculiarity is always hated and, when in the wrong, laughed at. You simply destroy respect for your taste rather than do harm to the object of your blame, and are left alone, you and your bad taste. If you cannot find the good in a thing, hide your incapacity and do not damn it right away. As a general rule bad taste springs from want of knowledge. What all say, is so, or will be so.

· 271 ·

IN EVERY OCCUPATION, IF YOU KNOW LITTLE STICK TO THE SAFE PATH. If you are not respected as subtle, you will be regarded as sure. On the other hand, someone well trained can plunge in and act as he pleases. To know little and yet seek danger is no different than to seek ruin. Follow the right hand, for what has gone before can be followed after. Let those with little knowledge keep to the king's highway, and in every case, knowing or unknowing, security is shrewder than uniqueness.

· 272 ·

SELL THINGS WITH A TARIFF OF COURTESY. You oblige people most that way. The bid of an interested buyer will never equal the return gift of a grateful recipient of a favor. Courtesy does not really make presents, but lays people under obligation, and generosity is the great obligation. To the right-minded nothing costs more dear than what is given to him. You sell it to him twice and for two prices: one for the value, one for the politeness. At the same time, it is true that with vulgar souls generosity is gibberish, for they do not understand the language of good breeding.

· 273 ·

COMPREHEND THE DISPOSITIONS OF THE PEOPLE YOU DEAL WITH. Then you will know their intentions. Cause known, effect known; beforehand in the disposition and after in the motive. The melancholy person always foresees misfortunes, the backbiter scandals—having no conception of the good, evil offers itself to them. A person moved by passion always speaks of things as different from what they are; it is his passion that speaks, not his reason. Thus each speaks as his feeling or his humor prompts him, and all far from the truth. Learn how to decipher faces and spell out the soul in the features. If someone always laughs set him down as foolish, if never as false. Beware of the gossip—he is either a babbler or a spy. Expect little good from the misshapen: they generally take revenge on nature, and do little honor to her, as she has done little to them. Beauty and folly generally go hand in hand.

· 274 ·

BE ATTRACTIVE. It is the magic of subtle courtesy. Use the magnet of your pleasant qualities more to attract goodwill than good deeds, but apply it to all. Merit is not enough unless supported by grace, which is the sole thing that gives general acceptance, and the most practical means of rule over others. To be in vogue is a matter of luck, yet it can be encouraged by skill, for art can best take root on a soil favored by nature. There goodwill grows and develops into universal favor.

· 275 ·

JOIN IN THE GAME AS FAR AS DECENCY PERMITS. Do not always pose and be a bore—this is a maxim for gallant bearing. You may yield a touch of dignity to gain the general goodwill. You may now and then go where most go, yet not beyond the bounds of decorum. He who makes a fool of himself in public will not be regarded as discreet in private life. One may lose more on a day of pleasure than has been gained during a whole life of labor. Still you must not always keep away; to be eccentric is to condemn all others. Still less act prudish—leave that to its appropriate sex—even religious prudery is ridiculous. Nothing so becomes a man as to be a man. A woman may affect a manly bearing as an excellence, but not vice versa.

· 276 ·

KNOW HOW TO RENEW YOUR CHARACTER BOTH WITH NATURE AND WITH ART. Every seven years the disposition changes, they say. Let it be a change for the better and for the nobler in your taste. After the first seven comes reason, with each succeeding lustre let a new excellence be added. Observe this change so as to aid it, and hope also for betterment in others. Hence it happens that many change their behavior when they change their position or their occupation. At times the change is not noticed till it reaches the height of maturity. At twenty a man is a peacock, at thirty a lion, at forty a camel, at fifty a serpent, at sixty a dog, at seventy an ape, at eighty nothing at all.

· 277 ·

DISPLAY YOURSELF. It is the illumination of talents. For each there comes an appropriate moment—use it, for not every day comes to triumph. There are some dashing men who make a show with little and others who make a whole exhibition with much. If ability to display them is joined to versatile gifts, they are regarded as miraculous. There are whole nations given to display; the Spanish people take the highest rank in this. Light was the first thing to cause creation to shine forth. Display fills up much, supplies much, and gives a second existence to things, especially when combined with real excellence. Heaven, which grants perfection, also provides the means of display, for one without the other is fruitless. Skill is, however, needed for display. Even excellence depends on circumstances and is not always opportune. Ostentation is out of place when it is out of time. More than any other quality it should be free of any affectation. If not, it is an offense, for it then borders on vanity and so on contempt. It must be moderate to avoid being vulgar, and any excess is despised by the wise. At times it consists in a sort of mute eloquence, a careless display of excellence. For a wise concealment is often the most effective boast, since the very withdrawal from view piques curiosity to the highest. It is a fine subtlety too, not to display one's excellence all at one time, but to grant stolen glances at it, more and more as time goes on. Each exploit should be the pledge of a greater, and applause at the first should only die away in expectation of its sequel.

· 278 ·

AVOID NOTORIETY IN ALL THINGS. Even excellences become defects if they become notorious. Notoriety arises from eccentricity, which is always blamed: he that is singular is left severely alone. Even beauty is discredited by foolish excess, which offends by the very notice it attracts. Still more does this apply to discreditable eccentricities. Yet among the wicked there are some that seek to be known for seeking novelties in vice so as to attain to the fame of infamy. Even in matters of the intellect lack of moderation may degenerate into empty talk.

· 279 ·

DO NOT RESPOND TO THOSE WHO CONTRADICT YOU. You have to distinguish whether the contradiction comes from cunning or from vulgarity. It is not always obstinacy, but may be artfulness. Notice this, for in the first case one may get into difficulties, in the other into danger. Caution is never more needed than against spies. There is no such countercheck to the picklock of the mind as to leave the key of caution in the inside lock of the door.

· 280 ·

BE TRUSTWORTHY. Honorable dealing is at an end, trusts are denied, few keep their word, the greater the service the poorer the reward—that is the way of the world nowadays. There are whole nations inclined to false dealing; with some treachery has always to be feared, with others breach of promise, with others deceit. Yet this bad behavior of others should be a warning to us rather than an example. The fear is that the sight of such unworthy behavior will override our integrity. But a person of honor should never forget what he is because he sees what others are.

· 281 ·

FIND FAVOR WITH PEOPLE OF GOOD SENSE. The tepid *yes* from a remarkable person is worth more than all the applause of the vulgar—you cannot make a meal off the smoke of chaff. The wise speak with understanding and their praise gives permanent satisfaction. The sage Antigonus reduced the theater of his fame to Zeus alone, and Plato called Aristotle his whole school. Some strive to fill their stomach albeit only with the breath of the mob. Even monarchs have need of authors, and fear their pens more than ugly women the painter's pencil.

· 282 ·

MAKE USE OF ABSENCE TO MAKE YOURSELF MORE ESTEEMED OR VALUED. If the accustomed presence diminishes fame, absence augments it. Someone that is regarded as a lion in his absence may be laughed at when present like the ridiculous offspring of the mighty. Talents get soiled by use, for it is easier to see the exterior rind than the kernel of greatness it encloses. Imagination reaches farther than sight. Disillusion, which ordinarily comes through the ears, also goes out through the ears. He keeps his fame that keeps himself in the center of public opinion. Even the phoenix uses its retirement for new adornment and turns absence into desire.

· 283 ·

HAVE THE GIFT OF DISCOVERY. It is a proof of the highest genius, yet when was genius without a touch of madness? If discovery be a gift of genius, choice is a mark of sound sense. Discovery comes by special grace and very seldom. For many can follow up a thing when found, but to find it first is the gift of the few—the first in excellence and in age. Novelty flatters, and if successful gives the possessor double credit. In matters of judgment novelties are dangerous because they lead to paradox, in matters of genius they deserve all praise. Yet both equally deserve applause if successful.

· 284 ·

DO NOT BE BURDENSOME. Then you will not be slighted. Respect yourself if you would have others respect you. Be sooner sparing than lavish with your presence. You will thus become desired and so well received. Never come unasked and only go when sent for. If you undertake a thing of your own accord you get all the blame if it fails, none of the thanks if it succeeds. Those who do not mind their own business are always the butt of blame, and because they thrust themselves in without shame they are thrust out with it.

· 285 ·

NEVER DIE OF ANOTHER'S BAD LUCK. Notice those who stick in the mud, and observe how they call others to their aid so as to console themselves with a companion in misfortune. They seek someone to help them to bear misfortune, and often those who turned the cold shoulder on them in prosperity now give them a helping hand. There is great caution needed in helping the drowning without endangering oneself.

· 286 ·

DO NOT BECOME RESPONSIBLE FOR ALL OR FOR EVERYONE. Otherwise you become a slave and the slave of all. Some are born more fortunate than others; they are born to do good as others are to receive it. Freedom is more precious than any gifts for which you may be tempted to give it up. Lay less stress on making many dependent on you than on keeping yourself independent of any. The sole advantage of power is that you can do more good. Above all do not regard a responsibility as a favor, for generally it is another's plan to make you dependent on him.

· 287 ·

NEVER ACT OUT OF PASSION. If you do all is lost. You cannot act for yourself if you are not yourself, and passion always drives out reason. In such cases interpose a prudent go-between who can keep cool. That is why onlookers see more of the game, because they keep cool. As soon as you notice that you are losing your temper beat a wise retreat. For no sooner is the blood up than it is spilled. A few moments may be given for many days' repentance for oneself and complaints from others.

· 288 ·

LIVE FOR THE MOMENT. Our acts and thoughts and all must be determined by circumstances. Act when you may, for time and tide wait for no one. Do not live by certain fixed rules, except those that relate to the cardinal virtues. Nor let your will pledge to fixed conditions, for you may have to drink the water tomorrow that you cast away today. There are some so absurdly paradoxical that they expect all the circumstances of an action should bend to their eccentric whims and not vice versa. The wise man knows that the very polestar of prudence lies in steering by the prevailing wind.

· 289 ·

NOTHING DEPRECIATES A PERSON MORE THAN TO SHOW HE IS JUST LIKE ANYONE ELSE. The day he is seen to be all too human he ceases to be thought divine. Frivolity is the exact opposite of reputation. And as the reserved are held to be more than men, so the frivolous are held to be less. No failing causes such failure of respect. For frivolity is the exact opposite of solid seriousness. A person of levity cannot be a person of weight even when he is old, and age should oblige him to be prudent. Although this blemish is so common it is nonetheless despised.

· 290 ·

IT IS A PIECE OF GOOD FORTUNE TO COMBINE PEOPLE'S LOVE AND RESPECT. Generally, one dare not be liked if one would be respected. Love is more sensitive than hate. Love and honor do not go well together. So that one should aim neither to be much feared nor much loved. Love introduces confidence, and the further this advances the more respect recedes. Prefer to be loved with respect rather than with passion, for that is a love suitable for many.

· 291 ·

KNOW HOW TO TEST PEOPLE. The care of the wise must guard against the snare of the wicked. Great judgment is needed to test the judgment of another. It is more important to know the characteristics and properties of people than those of vegetables and minerals. Indeed, it is one of the shrewdest things in life. You can tell metals by their ring and men by their voice. Words are proof of integrity, deeds still more. Here one requires extraordinary care, deep observation, subtle discernment, and judicious decision.

· 292 ·

LET YOUR PERSONAL QUALITIES SURPASS THE REQUIREMENTS OF YOUR OFFICE. Do not let it be the other way about. However high the post, the person should be higher. An extensive capacity expands and dilates more and more as his office becomes higher. On the other hand, the narrow-minded will easily lose heart and come to grief with diminished responsibilities and reputation. The great Augustus thought more of being a great man than a great prince. Here a lofty mind finds fit place, and well-grounded confidence finds its opportunity.

· 293 ·

MATURITY. It is shown in the costume, still more in the customs. Material weight is the sign of a precious metal, moral weight is the sign of a precious man. Maturity gives finish to his capacity and arouses respect. A composed bearing in a person forms a facade to his soul. It does not consist in the insensibility of fools, as frivolity would have it, but in a calm tone of authority. With people of this kind sentences are orations and acts are deeds. Maturity puts a finish on a person for each is so far complete only according as he possesses maturity. On ceasing to be a child a person begins to gain seriousness and authority.

· 294 ·

BE MODERATE IN YOUR VIEWS. Everyone holds views according to his interest, and imagines he has abundant grounds for them. For with most people judgment has to give way to inclination. It may occur that two may meet with exactly opposite views and yet each thinks to have reason on his side, yet reason is always true to itself and never has two faces. In such a situation a prudent person will proceed with care, for his judgment of his opponent's view may cast doubt on his own. Place yourself in the other person's place and then investigate the reasons for his opinion. You will not then condemn him or justify yourself in such a confusing way.

· 295 ·

DO NOT AFFECT WHAT YOU HAVE NOT EFFECTED. Many claim accomplishments without the slightest cause. With great coolness they make a mystery of all. Chameleons of applause they afford others a surfeit of laughter. Vanity is always objectionable, here it is despicable. These ants of honor go crawling about filching scraps of exploits. The greater your exploits the less you need affect them. Content yourself with doing, leave the talking to others. Give away your deeds but do not sell them. And do not hire venal pens to write down praises in the mud, to the derision of those who know better. Aspire rather to be a hero than merely to appear to be one.

· 296 ·

NOBLE QUALITIES. Noble qualities make noble people; a single one of them is worth more than a multitude of mediocre ones. There was once a man who made all his belongings, even his household utensils, as great as possible. How much more ought a great man see that the qualities of his soul are as great as possible. In God all is eternal and infinite;

in a hero everything should be great and majestic, so that all his deeds—
no, all his words—should be pervaded by a transcendent majesty.

· 297 ·

ALWAYS ACT AS IF OTHERS WERE WATCHING. He must see all round
who sees that men see him or will see him. He knows that walls have
ears and that ill deeds rebound back. Even when alone he acts as if the
eyes of the whole world were upon him. For as he knows that sooner
or later all will be known, so he considers those to be present as wit-
nesses who must afterwards hear of the deed. He that wished the whole
world might always see him did not mind that his neighbors could see
him over their walls.

· 298 ·

THREE THINGS GO TO A PRODIGY. They are the choicest gifts of Heav-
en's perfections—a fertile genius, a profound intellect, a pleasant and
refined taste. To think well is good, to think right is better—it is the
understanding of the good. It will not do for the judgment to reside in
the backbone; it would be of more trouble than use. To think right is
the fruit of a reasonable nature. At twenty the will rules, at thirty the
intellect, at forty the judgment. There are minds that shine in the dark
like the eyes of the lynx, and are most clear where there is most darkness. Others are more adapted for the occasion—they always hit on that
which suits the emergency; such a quality produces much and good—a
sort of fertile felicity. In the meantime, good taste seasons the whole of
life.

· 299 ·

LEAVE OFF HUNGRY. One ought to remove even the bowl of nectar
from the lips. Demand is the measure of value. Even with regard to

bodily thirst it is a mark of good taste to slake but not to quench it. Little and good is twice good. The second time around comes as a great falling off. Too much pleasure is always dangerous and brings down the ill-will of the highest powers. The only way to please is to revive the appetite by the hunger that is left. If you must excite desire, better do it by the impatience of want than by the surfeit of enjoyment. Happiness earned gives double joy.

· 300 ·

IN ONE WORD, BE A SAINT. So is all said at once. Virtue is the link of all perfections, the center of all the felicities. She makes a person prudent, discreet, sagacious, cautious, wise, courageous, thoughtful, trustworthy, happy, honored, truthful, and a universal hero. Three things make a person happy—health, holiness, and wisdom. Virtue is the sun of our world, and has for its course a good conscience. She is so beautiful that she finds favor with both God and man. Nothing is lovable but virtue, nothing detestable but vice. A person's capacity and greatness are to be measured by his virtue and not by his fortune. She alone is all-sufficient. She makes people lovable in life, memorable after death.

MAXIMS

1. Everything is at its peak of perfection.
2. Character and intellect.
3. Keep matters for a time in suspense.
4. Knowledge and courage.
5. Make people depend on you.
6. A person at his peak.
7. Avoid outshining your superiors.
8. Be without passions.
9. Avoid the faults of your nation.
10. Fortune and fame.
11. Cultivate relationships with those who can teach you.
12. Nature and art, material and workmanship.
13. Act sometimes on second thoughts, sometimes on first impulse.
14. The thing itself and the way it is done.
15. Keep auxiliary wits around you.
16. Knowledge and good intentions.
17. Vary your mode of action.
18. Application and ability.
19. Arouse no exaggerated expectations when you start something.
20. A man of the times.
21. The art of being lucky.
22. Knowledge has a purpose.
23. Be free of imperfection.

24. Keep your imagination under control.

25. Know how to take a hint.

26. Find out each person's thumbscrew.

27. Prize intensity more than extent.

28. Be common in nothing.

29. Be a person of integrity.

30. Have nothing to do with disreputable occupations.

31. Select the lucky and avoid the unlucky.

32. Have a reputation for being gracious.

33. Know how to withdraw.

34. Know your strongest quality.

35. Think things over, especially those that are most important.

36. Before acting or refraining, weigh your luck.

37. Keep a store of sarcasms and know how to use them.

38. Leave your luck while still winning.

39. Recognize when things are ripe, and know how to enjoy them.

40. Gain people's goodwill.

41. Never exaggerate.

42. Natural leadership.

43. Think with the few and speak with the many.

44. Sympathy with great minds.

45. Use, but do not abuse, cunning.

46. Master your antipathies.

47. Avoid incurring obligations.

48. So much depends on being a person of depth.

49. Be a person of observation and judgment.

50. Never lose your self-respect.

51. Know how to choose well.

52. Never be upset.

53. Be diligent and intelligent.

54. Know how to show your strength.

55. Know how to wait.

56. Have presence of mind.

57. Be slow and sure.

58. Adapt yourself to those around you.

59. Finish off well.

60. Have sound judgment.

61. Excel in what is excellent.

62. Use good instruments.

63. To be the first of the kind is excellent.

64. Avoid worry.

65. Cultivate taste.

66. See to it that things end well.

67. Choose an occupation that wins distinction.

68. It is better to help with intelligence than with memory.

69. Do not give way to every common impulse.

70. Know how to say "no."

71. Do not vacillate.

72. Be resolute.

73. Know how to use evasion.

74. Do not be unapproachable.

75. Chose a heroic ideal.

76. Do not always be joking.

77. Be all things to all people.

78. The art of undertaking things.

79. A jovial disposition.

80. Take care when you get information.

81. Renew your brilliance.

82. Drain nothing to the dregs, neither good nor bad.

83. Allow yourself some forgivable sin.

84. Make use of your enemies.

85. Do not be a wild card, a jack-of-all-trades.

86. Prevent scandal.

87. Culture and elegance.

88. Let your behavior be fine and noble.

89. Know yourself.

90. The secret of long life.

91. Never set to work at anything if you have any doubts about its prudence.

92. Transcendent wisdom.

93. Versatility.

94. Keep the extent of your abilities unknown.

95. Keep expectation alive.

96. The highest discretion.

97. Obtain and preserve a reputation.

98. Write your intentions in cypher.

99. Reality and appearance.

100. Be a person without illusions, one who is wise and righteous, a philosophical courtier.

101. One half of the world laughs at the other, and fools are they all.

102. Be able to stomach big slices of luck.

103. Let each keep up his dignity.

104. Get to know what is needed in different occupations.

105. Do not be a bore.

106. Do not parade your position.

107. Show no self-satisfaction.

108. The shortest path to greatness is along with others.

109. Do not be censorious.

110. Do not wait till you are a setting sun.

111. Have friends.

112. Gain goodwill.

113. In times of prosperity prepare for adversity.

114. Never compete.

115. Get used to the failings of those around you.

116. Only act with honorable people.

117. Never talk about yourself.

118. Acquire the reputation for courtesy.

119. Avoid becoming disliked.

120. Live practically.

121. Do not make much ado about nothing.

122. Distinction in speech and action.

123. Avoid affectation.

124. Make yourself sought after.

125. Do not be a blacklister of other people's faults.

126. Folly consists not in committing folly, but in not hiding it when committed.

127. Grace in everything.

128. Highmindedness.

129. Never complain.

130. Do and be seen doing.

131. Nobility of feeling.

132. Revise your judgments.

133. Better mad with the rest of the world than wise alone.

134. Double your resources.

135. Do not nourish the spirit of contradiction.

136. Post yourself in the center of things.

137. The sage should be self-sufficient.

138. The art of letting things alone.

139. Recognize unlucky days.

140. Find the good in a thing at once.

141. Do not listen to yourself.

142. Never from obstinacy take the wrong side because your opponent has anticipated you by taking the right one.

143. Never become paradoxical in order to avoid being trite.

144. Begin with another's to end with your own.

145. Do not show your wounded finger, for everything will knock up against it.

146. Look into the interior of things.

147. Do not be inaccessible.

148. Have the art of conversation.

149. Know how to put off ills on others.

150. Know how to get your price for things.

151. Think beforehand.

152. Never have a companion who outshines you.

153. Beware of entering where there is a great gap to be filled.

154. Do not believe, or like, lightly.

155. The art of mastering your passions.

156. Select your friends.

157. Do not make mistakes about character.

158. Make use of your friends.

159. Put up with fools.

160. Be careful in speaking.

161. Know your pet faults.

162. How to triumph over your rivals and detractors.

163. Never—out of sympathy with the unfortunate—involve yourself in their fate.

164. Throw straws in the air to test the wind.

165. Wage war honorably.

166. Distinguish people of words from people of deeds.

167. Know how to rely on yourself.

168. Do not indulge in the eccentricities of folly.

169. Be more careful not to miss once than to hit a hundred times.

170. In all things keep something in reserve.

171. Do not waste influence.

172. Never contend with someone who has nothing to lose.

173. Do not be made of glass in your relations with others, still less in friendship.

174. Do not live in a hurry.

175. A solid person.

176. Have knowledge, or know those who do.

177. Avoid being too familiar with others.

178. Trust your heart.

179. Reticence is the seal of capacity.

180. Never guide the enemy to what he has to do.

181. The truth, but not the whole truth.

182. A grain of boldness in everything.

183. Do not hold your views too firmly.

184. Do not stand on ceremony.

185. Never stake your credit on a single cast of the dice.

186. Recognize faults, however highly placed.

187. Do pleasant things yourself, unpleasant things through others.

188. Be the bearer of praise.

189. Utilize another's wants.

190. Find consolation in all things.

191. Do not take payment in politeness.

192. A peaceful life is a long life.

193. Watch out for people who begin with another's concern to end with their own.

194. Have reasonable views of yourself and of your affairs.

195. Know how to appreciate.

196. Know your ruling star.

197. Do not carry fools on your back.

198. Know how to transplant yourself.

199. Find your proper place by merit, not by presumption.

200. Leave something to wish for.

201. They are all fools who seem so, as well as half the rest.

202. Words and deeds make the perfect person.

203. Know the great people of your age.

204. Attempt easy tasks as if they were difficult and difficult as if they were easy.

205. Know how to play the card of contempt.

206. Know that there are vulgar people everywhere.

207. Be moderate.

208. Do not die of the fools' disease.

209. Keep yourself free from common follies.

210. Know how to play the card of truth.

211. In heaven all is bliss.

212. Keep to yourself the final touches of your art.

213. Know how to contradict.

214. Do not turn one blunder into two.

215. Watch out for those who act on second thoughts.

216. Be expressive.

217. Neither love nor hate forever.

218. Never act from obstinacy but from knowledge.

219. Do not pass for a hypocrite.

220. If you cannot clothe yourself in lion skin use fox pelt.

221. Do not seize occasions to embarrass yourself or others.

222. Reserve is proof of prudence.

223. Do not be eccentric, neither from affectation nor carelessness.

224. Never take things against the grain, no matter how they come.

225. Know your chief fault.

226. Take care to be obliging.

227. Do not be the slave of first impressions.

228. Do not be a scandalmonger.

229. Plan out your life wisely.

230. Open your eyes early.

231. Never let things be seen half-finished.

232. Have a touch of business sense.

233. Do not let the morsels you offer be distasteful.

234. Never trust your honor to another, unless you have his in pledge.

235. Know how to ask.

236. Make an obligation beforehand of what would have to be a reward afterward.

237. Never share the secrets of your superiors.

238. Know what is lacking in yourself.

239. Do not be overly critical.

240. Make use of folly.

241. Put up with mockery but do not practice it yourself.

242. Push advantages.

243. Do not be too much of a dove.

244. Create a feeling of obligation.

245. Have original and out-of-the-way views.

246. Never offer satisfaction unless it is demanded.

247. Know a little more, live a little less.

248. Do not go with the latest speaker.

249. Never begin life with what should end it.

250. When to turn conversation around.

251. Use human means as if there were no divine ones, and divine means as if there were no human ones.

252. Neither belong entirely to yourself nor entirely to others.

253. Do not explain too much.

254. Never despise an evil, however small.

255. Do good a little at a time, but often.

256. Go prepared.

257. Never let matters come to a breaking point.

258. Find someone to share your troubles with.

259. Anticipate injuries and turn them into favors.

260. We belong to no one and no one to us, entirely.

261. Do not follow up a folly.

262. Be able to forget.

263. Many things of taste one should not possess oneself.

264. Have no careless days.

265. Set difficult tasks for those under you.

266. Do not become bad from sheer goodness.

267. Silken words, sugared manners.

268. The wise do at once what the fool does later.

269. Make use of the novelty of your position.

270. Do not condemn alone that which pleases all.

271. In every occupation, if you know little stick to the safe path.

272. Sell things with a tariff of courtesy.

273. Comprehend the dispositions of the people you deal with.

274. Be attractive.

275. Join in the game as far as decency permits.

276. Know how to renew your character both with nature and with art.

277. Display yourself.

278. Avoid notoriety in all things.

279. Do not respond to those who contradict you.

280. Be trustworthy.

281. Find favor with people of good sense.

282. Make use of absence to make yourself more esteemed or valued.

283. Have the gift of discovery.

284. Do not be burdensome.

285. Never die of another's bad luck.

286. Do not become responsible for all or for everyone.

287. Never act out of passion.

288. Live for the moment.

289. Nothing depreciates a person more than to show he is just like anyone else.

290. It is a piece of good fortune to combine people's love and respect.

291. Know how to test people.

292. Let your personal qualities surpass the requirements of your office.

293. Maturity.

294. Be moderate in your views.

295. Do not affect what you have not effected.

296. Noble qualities.

297. Always act as if others were watching.

298. Three things go to a prodigy.

299. Leave off hungry.

300. In one word, be a saint.

PLACE
STAMP
HERE

SHAMBHALA PUBLICATIONS, INC.

MAILING LIST
P.O. BOX 308, BACK BAY ANNEX
BOSTON, MASSACHUSETTS 02117-0308

SHAMBHALA

SHAMBHALA

If you wish to receive a copy of the latest Shambhala Publications catalogue of books and to be placed on our mailing list, please send us this card—or send us an e-mail at info@shambhala.com

Please print

BOOK IN WHICH THIS CARD WAS FOUND ....

NAME ....

ADDRESS ....

CITY .... STATE ....

ZIP OR POSTAL CODE ....

COUNTRY (*if outside U.S.A.*) ....

Detach bookmark before mailing card.

Shambhala Classics

THE ART OF WORLDLY WISDOM
by Baltasar Gracián, translated by Joseph Jacobs

THE BOOK OF FIVE RINGS
by Miyamoto Musashi, translated by Thomas Cleary

NARROW ROAD TO THE INTERIOR
and Other Writings
by Matsuo Bashō, translated by Sam Hamill

THE RUMI COLLECTION
*An Anthology of Translation of
Mevlâna Jalâluddin Rumi*
edited by Kabir Helminski

SIDDHARTHA
by Hermann Hesse, translated by Sherab Chödzin Kohn

T'AI CHI CLASSICS
translated with commentary by Waysun Liao

THE TIBETAN BOOK OF THE DEAD
*The Great Liberation through
Hearing in the Bardo*
translated with commentary by
Francesca Fremantle and Chögyam Trungpa

WHEN THINGS FALL APART
Heart Advice for Difficult Times
by Pema Chödrön